Love requires *Sacrifice.*

Repetition is the mother of all learning.

Love Heals
Love Heals
Love Heals
Love Heals
Love Heals
Love Heals
Love Heals
Love Heals
Love Heals
Love Heals
Love Heals
Love Heals

Repetition is the mother of all learning.

LOVE HEALS

Parents care for

children as they develop

into young adults

There is a time the

grown children

may need to care for

parents….

Visualize someone caring for you.

In turn, give your charge the kind of treatment you would expect!

The Walker Family 1950

Marsha, Marjorie, Risdom, Morris and Lesley

Every day thousands of men and women in the United States turn sixty-five.

Who will help them?

Will anyone help them?

Marjorie Grace Phillips Walker 65 years old.

Think about it!

Being lonely and helpless

are two major problems

for senior citizens.

Why should you help?

Because…..

You are looking at

<u>YOU</u>

in the future!

Think about that!
It happens quickly.

LESSONS OF LOVE

Lovingly written by

Marsha J. O'Brien

TABLE OF CONTENTS

Preface   19

1. Acceptance   31

2. Two Steps Ahead of the Game   48

3. An Inside Look from the Inside   68

4. How to Fill the Cup   89

5. What if She's Bossy Whiney and Rude?   141

6. A Reason to Live   174

7. Ascension   192

8. Bottom of the Barrel, the Top of the Line   218

9. The Last Goodbye   289

10. Tragedy to Triumph   302

11. Reflections   330

12. Legacy of Love   378

13. Tomorrow   422

Addendum   444

Within these pages you will notice larger print and more spacing between paragraphs.

This was done intentionally to those with reading challenges, for better comprehension, and a more enjoyable read.

Preface

Today could be the day your life changes FOREVER. This book lovingly shares events that took place when I was the caregiver for my mother. It was an unexpected event becoming a caregiver. It took trial and error to finally really become the caregiver that my mother deserved.

Care "giving" is one of the fastest growing unpaid professions in the United States. According to the National Alliance for Care Giving, during the past year more than sixty-seven million Americans provided care to a family member, friend, or loved one, many of whom are suffering from different stages of Alzheimer's disease, dementia, or some other age-related problems.

If you become a care giver, you get swept up in a flurry of tasks. You make decisions for others about things you yourself have not considered before. You will attempt to manage behavioral problems, make arrangements for medical care, be responsible for transportation, shopping, cooking, and feeding the person. Meanwhile you will be coping with your own responsibilities, anxieties and fears.

You may after a few months wonder how you can keep the commitment of caring for this person while not losing your own mind.

Though I have written primarily about caring for an elderly woman, because I did for over ten years, everything can certainly be applied to a male recipient. Men grow old and need help too, so many things you will discover here can be used to help the elderly man in your life – whether it be your father, a grandfather, or just a gentleman you choose to help.

This book will help you learn how to care give effectively. You want to come out of this job loving and sane. You want to make the person you are caring for have as much fun as possible, and have as good of health as possible during the time of their withering on the vine. These will be their last days and you do not want to regret a thing. We humans have a tendency to play the reel of our mistakes over and over in our minds, sometimes for decades.

It is possible to be successful. I cared for my mama for almost ten years and learned so much during that time. She learned lessons too and I must say, I have had few regrets in the fulfilling of my job as a caregiver with mama. She deserves credit too as she was an unusually strong minded and spiritual woman. It is only with aging and overwhelming pain myself that I realize I only thought I understood her pain. I hadn't a clue.

We both learned lessons of love in one of the hardest jobs we both had to endure in our lifetimes.

<u>Changing demographics means that demand for care giving the elderly is projected to increase by 48 percent the next decade. It will create 1,600,000 unpaid caretaking positions.</u>

Statistics reflect a startling number of people who are now finding themselves in the position of care giving an elderly person, whether related or not.

Baby boomers are turning sixty-five by the thousands, every day.

There are many pre-teen children who are put into a position of being a caregiver, perhaps for a grandma or grandpa, simply because there is no one else to do it.

<u>Many home care workers do receive compensation from different organizations and states.</u> The Department of Labor recently issued home care workers basic federal wage and hour protections. So much more needs to be done.

My family thinks I did a splendid job.

To this day I reflect and feel there were so many other things I could have done to make Mama's life exquisite and my life less traumatic. I often complained to others how exhausted I was, and how I wished more help had been available. God loves a cheerful giver, and sometimes I felt too exhausted to be cheerful.

I should have been a cheerful giver all then \\time, but I but just did not know how to…THEN.

The point is this: if you give reluctantly or under compulsion, it is far different in delivery than if you give bountifully and from the heart. Decide in your heart this job is really a way to honor your parent. If you find yourself in this position, give in to it happily and with a full heart. Do not hesitate and grumble and complain. The results you will see with negative emotions, are far less effective for your mama, and will ultimately make you less happy too.

Resentment will grow and ineffective care giving will be what you reap. Mama always told me that love means sacrifice. I came to discover that my small sacrifices were a tribute to her entire life and her pending departure. It was well worth the challenge.

Include your family in offering help. It will challenge and satisfy children and young adults on so many levels. Their young education will broaden exponentially.

We have only touched first base about the specifics such as when it is time to take the car keys away, have your family member move to a residential care home, move a family member to your own home, or exerting a bit of forceful conversation to minimize catastrophic events.

The physical care may include showering and dressing your charge. It could include l lengthy phone calls if the recipient is still living alone. You may have to rearrange the home of your mama or the person you care for so that their safety is not at risk for a fall or worse. You may have to transport a wheelchair, or rearrange your time schedule.

YOU CAN DO IT! Make it the challenge of your lifetime and when the job is done, your heart and your life will be better for the experience. I promise!

Acceptance

Chapter 1

Acceptance

There are many reasons you need to find acceptance of this position early on. If you find yourself in the position of becoming a caregiver for someone you love, and cannot change it, the only thing you can do is ACCEPT IT!

Lessons in this chapter remind you that you must accept the job and trust that God, or providence, and to know that there is still something for you in the future. But now is the time you must sacrifice in the name of love.

If you are caring for your mother or father, remember how much you love them. Try to always keep this in mind.

When Mama and I first realized she needed help on a regular basis she was MAD. She was still fiercely independent and she was mad at herself. She did not want to be a burden on any member of her family.

I remember she said "I never thought I would be a feeble old lady, falling all over the place, with people having to take time out of their lives to help me. It makes me sick. I worked all of my life and did the best I could, and what is my reward? I have lots of wrinkles and lots of pain, all the time. I cannot believe this has happened to me.

What did I ever do wrong?"

If there is no other option, no other help in the family available, you had better find acceptance with a good attitude. You do not want to spend the rest of your life regretting your choices or resenting the person you are caring for until someone comes to help - or the death of this person.

I am ashamed to admit I fought it fiercely inside for much of the time I was her caregiver. I am equally glad to say she never knew the battle I was having over the demands made on my life and the loss of freedom. She also did not realize the difficulty of being in the position of a caregiver for your own beloved mother.

It was difficult to see her diminish.

She was a beautiful soul who was

withering on the vine.

The realization Mama and I had to arrive at

was this: This is Life. This was the scenario

we faced. We had to fight it or accept it.

I began a career in fitness and counseling

twenty years ago so I could help people get

on the preventive side of medicine and illness.

I loved helping people get strong and healthy.

Why not help my own mother? The only

other choice was a home for the elderly, and

that had always been Mama's nightmare.

Mama finally admitted she needed help and

was grateful for every moment I dedicated to

helping her, whether it was taking her to the doctor, shopping, or to the hairdresser for her weekly outing to visit with the girls.

Initially I did accept the position. I loved Mama. I wanted to help. I just didn't know what to expect or if I could handle the future.

Being a novice, I did not know what in the world I was doing anyway. Like the parent and first newborn, we would learn together. That is the way it was for Mama and me.

It was very difficult to accept the fact this was to be solely my job for all the years Mama was alive in the future. It was not what I had planned.

I wanted freedom to travel with my husband. I wanted to have freedom to have fun and enjoy these years as a woman with grown children, on her own once again.

When my father died, my twin brother and my sister agreed we would share the responsibility of caring for Mama if it became necessary.

Morris and Lynn were in the midst of traveling on the road with the kids in their Earthwalker family band. They talked about family, the environment, and gave thousands of kiddos an education on love, right and wrong, and lots of humor!

As the weeks and months came and left, as the injuries and doctor appointments increased, as the workload increased and the time to rest and regenerate became less and less, my resentment grew-and it was only because I was exhausted. It was not towards Mama. She felt terrible having to ask for help.

Instead, I resented my siblings. I felt at the time that they should have been there to help and relieve me. What became crystal clear after months of feeling deserted by my family was that I was the one who was REALLY available!

My sister was living on the east coast and her plate was full. My twin brother was on the road trying to support his family.

My sis did fly from the east coast many times. God bless her for doing that when she could. Sometimes Mama would have preferred her time being independent. My sister could not have known though, as she was trying to help. Though my sis and mama did enjoy the visits very much though, sometimes the timing, it did not relieve much of the burden that I was carrying.

My brother's job depended on him traveling round the country and around the world. It was nearly impossible for him to visit often. I got over my resentment for it was really not justified to resent either one of them for living their lives and doing what needed to be done.

I had been praying for God to direct me to the path He wanted me to take for the future. When He did, I did not recognize it! I was not paying enough attention (or perhaps I simply was not fully accepting and trusting Him enough).

My husband and I moved Mama from the snow to a warm climate, and my family moved too. When mama began to need help, the children were grown and I was not working full-time.

I had put myself in the position of being close to her. I was her baby (only by 9 minutes) -nonetheless, her baby!

When Mama passed, I saw the pain of regret in my beloved sister and brother's eyes. They knew that they should have spent more time with Mama, but LIFE keeps us from fulfilling all obligations. They felt the pangs of knowing they had missed precious moments with Mama, and that they could never be recreated again.

I felt badly for their loss, and grateful for the experiences with Mama that I was able to share. She not only told me stories I'd never heard before, but in many ways, she gave me a head start on preparation for my old age.

When the pain was bad Mama was often nasty. Those feelings were multiplied on the bad days.

The good days revived the sweet little optimist who reminded me that there is not a difficulty that enough love will not conquer. With God in your heart, love is always there too.

There was one point I thought my mother would live another ten years. I remember complaining to someone that I was tired and didn't know how much longer I could keep this pace. It was all about me! Mama was dead within the week and I wished I had never even thought those thoughts.

It is tough seeing someone you love slip little by little under the years of hard life.
She was riddled with pain, and void of dreams or a future.

It is a challenge to keep current with your own affairs and still be the vivacious and positive force in the life of someone who feels her life has passed her.

Mama fought her own demons. She fought for her independence and the right to retain dignity. She fought senility and a physically debilitating disease. She fought nagging pain, boredom, and loneliness from the loss of her husband and most of her relatives. She fought to remain cheerful. She fought to find a reason to live.
She fought to find motivation to live even one day at a time. She never let the rest of the family know how she felt.

I find now as I walk in her shoes that even I could not understand the magnitude of her challenges and pain.

She braved these battles for the last ten years of her life and I cared for her throughout that time. In my caring for her, she taught me more than I have ever before learned about life. She gave me insight into my own future and courage to fight the battles we all will someday come to meet.

There are so many biases and slights toward the older population. The elderly are not a breed apart. When you look at an elderly person remember you are looking at yourself in the future.

We all have responsibilities we must complete. No matter how long our list of jobs to do is, it is important to remember when someone we love is gone from planet, it is as final as it gets. It is difficult not to take life for granted. We all do it, and someday, we will all be gone.

Remember what your mama has done for you. Think of what you do for your children.

Even if your relationship was less than perfect, no parent can raise a child without sacrifice and work.

Remember too when you say words, you give them life. Be careful not to say words you will regret.

There are no simple answers and there are no easy solutions. The choice is always in your hands to react to any situation in a positive manner.

If you accept the situation with grace, it will ease your pain and your mamas too. I promise.

I hope the writings on the next page will help you in your endeavor to be a good caregiver for your mama (or daddy, or step parent). We all need help at some point. Though you may find your "person" feisty, or determined to be on their own, you may have to just sit down and have an open discussion about your concerns.

"God grant me the serenity to accept the things I cannot change, the courage to change the things I can, and the wisdom to know the difference."

Karl Paul Reinhold Niebuhr

"I can do all things through Christ, which strengthens me."

Philippians 4:13

"Bear ye one another's burden, and so fulfill the law of Christ."

Galatians 6:2

Chapter 2

Chapter 2

Two Steps Ahead of the Game

Mama said to me "Getting older is tricky. It's the hardest job I have ever had, and I have had some pretty demanding positions. You have to be tough to age gracefully. You have to be a fighter."

How right she was.

One of the most important things we learned as we resolved and accepted taking this path together, was to always try to stay two steps ahead of the game.

There were plenty of surprises to catch us off guard so the things that we could plan and execute were of great help. Deciding what was necessary and what was not, proved to be one of our many, many challenges

When you have two grown women who have raised families, lived in and organized their own homes, and now have to plan life together, you have a balancing act to do.

I was fearful as time went by, that if more serious health problems occurred, she would not be able to afford prescriptions, surgery or any special care needs. Mama thought I was insane.
She had worked all of her life and never taken any form of what she called a handout.

She wasn't about to admit she was headed for the poorhouse. However, in the long run, I was right, and she admitted it was the right thing to have done. She had a right to get help. That is not wrong. That was not using the system. Daddy had died years earlier, and her only income was her social security.

Even with Medicare and other state benefits, our seniors still have to pay for dental work, and eye care. This is absolutely ludicrous in my eyes, as these are usually the first things to deteriorate! She said if she went to jail, she could get free everything - room and board, food, and all the things she needed to live happily and debt free. I still get furious that she had been absolutely correct.

We bantered back and forth for over two years before Mama agreed to apply for Medicare. She resented all the personal details she was forced to reveal. She was upset during the entire process. It is easier to understand now why she so resented this step.

We will expound on humiliation and pride lessons later in this book. They are volatile and important emotions that are right smack in the middle of this aging process.

A year or so after Medicare kicked in, Mama caught me by the arm and grabbed my hand and squeezed it three times (an old family tradition that meant I love you). She looked at me with her beautiful blue eyes and said,

"Thanks for insisting on this help honey. I truly do not know what I would have done without it. I'm am so sorry I made such a fuss."

It certainly did not matter by then, and I told her so, but it was hell during the application and waiting period!

She was so grateful I had applied for a parking placard for her. She has severe osteoporosis throughout her little body that made it very difficult for her to walk too far.

Many older folks would probably benefit someone mentioning that it is possible to get parking privileges if needed.

I can honestly say I never took advantage of using the placard for my own comfort. I cannot say that for all people. I have scene a few people who used the space just to be lazy and get a closer spot. There is a fine line for those who choose to take that chance, as there is quite a fine if they are caught.

The worst of it in my mind is the thought of someone who is really in need, not being able to find a parking space. Mama just would have had to totally change her plans if she was not able to park close in.

There are so many ways to save your mother from unnecessary discomfort and any inconvenience.

Equipment to make life easier and safer for her may include a hospital bed, a special seat for the toilet, a wheelchair, a walker, a cane, or a tool Mama fondly called the grabber.

I am certainly not suggesting you get all that is available, but only those things that are necessary. Mama needed and used everything we ordered.

What I am suggesting is to think ahead so that you are prepared
for situations that subsequently will arise. Mama had fought using the walker and the wheelchair, and she hated the shower seat, but reluctantly she did use most all of the items we got for her.

I understand NOW why she fought it so hard. It was not using the items that bothered her. She was fighting to retain agility, dignity, and her last freedoms. No older person chooses to be dependent and trapped within the limitations of their own body.

She had to keep trying or loose what freedoms she still retained.

Then she would remember that she still enjoyed the company of the people who loved her, and she still loved the birds and the rain and the conversations between family and friends.

She wanted to keep her sanity.

There are many other services that may be available to help your mother. Many communities have someone deliver hot meals to the elderly, and those in need. The service is called Meals on Wheels and the cost in minimal.

Many seniors have lost the drive and desire to cook. The Golden Umbrella is a free service that guarantees they will at least have one hot and complete meal a day.

I think more than the meals, she loved the conversations she had with the gentleman who delivered her food. She actually began doing a little marital counseling for the young man. Just five minutes together and they both felt better.

Another website that sells custom homemade style meals is momsmeals.com.

It never occurred to me that a senior might become anorexic. Current studies have revealed that many seniors are indeed anorexic, lacking nutrition and energy because of too little food.

As people age often the appetite weans and eating alone may not seem appealing. Mama told me one time she was sick of every-thing she ate! That was a challenge to meet but we worked through it together.

You may decide to cook an extra portion when you cook for your family. It might be safer as well, as many elders are not really "safe" working in the kitchen any more.

They might not be physically up to it, or just careless about leaving the stove on, or something that could be dangerous in the long run.

Perhaps you could pick your mama up for dinner with the family at least once a week. Mama chose to live alone as long as she could, but if your parent lives with you, that would resolve that problem.

  There are also organizations that provide other services for seniors. These also allows them to have some social contact.
Most towns have senior centers that provide companionship and activities. Costs are kept

down, and the activities include bingo, art classes, perhaps country-dance, various card games, and a thorough catalog of fun things to do.

Most towns have senior centers that provide companionship and activities. Costs are kept down, and the activities include bingo, art classes, perhaps country-dance, various card games, and a thorough catalog of fun things to do.

In California the government is offering free forever phones to those with limited incomes, those on Medicaid or Medi-Cal, even those in retirement homes.

It is so important to make sure your parent is

not bored. With boredom comes loneliness, and loneliness can be life threatening.

One of the things that gave Mama great confidence was making sure she had a cell phone with her. I simply attached the phone case to her walker, and she knew she could call for help if needed. We also made sure emergency numbers were close. The cell phone became a friend for life.

There are organizations around the country subsidized by the government to help older citizens remain in their homes. It is actually less expensive for a senior to remain independent, but more importantly, they have a right to live a free life for as long as possible.

After a bit of research, we found a group that provided financial assistance with the rent each month, and the organization sent out workers to visit with clients and check on their needs. Almost as big a help to Mama was the introduction and friendship of those involved with the organizations.

It was Mama's idea, and a really good one, to make a chart of her medications, run off copies for each day, and then put those copies on the counter with a pen nearby. It was really an easy task then to keep track of the medications it was necessary for her to use.

She took out the proper dosage for each day and placed them in a small dish.

As each one was taken, she simply marked next to the place where the medication was listed. At the end of each day the bowl was empty and each medication checked off. It was great relief for both of us to know there would be no forgetting to take her meds, or over-doses, or lapses in between medications that would cause more pain.

Some medications have almost as much ramifications in side effects as they produce in helping. Any narcotic will cause some memory problems, perhaps dizziness, and absolutely constipation. This subject deserves to be discussed, as it is urgent to attend to keep your loved one strong and healthy.

There are many ways to help. Purchase stool softeners (100mg to 250mg per day). It is safe to take two pills a day, for a few weeks, in order to help the problem. The number one thing to do to help an older person to be healthy is to help them stay hydrated. Seniors seem to dismiss water as an important pathway to better health and a colon that works properly.

Encourage the person you are taking care of to keep bottles of water around the house so it will be easier for them to remember to stay hydrated, and more convenient.

My mama preferred glasses in the kitchen, bedroom and bathroom areas. Her water was good from the faucet so she was able to fill the glasses easily.

There are also other methods of keeping the body cleansed. Keep plenty of fruit in the home, including the old standby prunes and/or prune juice. And hydrate, hydrate, hydrate!

The job of being a caregiver, even part time, will increase stressful events in the lives of the caregivers. Anything that you can do to organize and simplify things will benefit all parties involved.

Remember for every change this position causes in your life, there is an equal change with less rewards, and less dreams in sight for your mama. The elderly may feel humiliated because their exterior is gradually deteriorating.

Quite often Mama felt ashamed of her body and face, and she retreated into seclusion to hide, which in turn, magnified her loneliness.

Try to keep the changes light and positive. For example, you might say, "I am so glad we could find this walker; it will be so great for you to be able to walk a bit further, and have more freedom in doing so." Or perhaps, "I am so proud of your ability to be flexible and try new things, and particularly with all the challenges you face already".

We all need to be appreciated and given accolades on occasion. Positive draws positive towards

Chapter 3

Chapter 3

In Inside Look from the Inside

In this chapter I share Mama's wisdom about aging. She taught me things that apply to us all, and now that I am a senior citizen, they have become crystal clear. Three things make us whole - our mind, body and spirit. We learn as we begin to get older, that these elements are really intertwined from within us.

One gift of aging is that is that the meaning of life is clearer, and our lists of priorities begin to change to seek out what is really important.

Another thing is that as we age, we find all the fuss about staying young is just to sell us on purchasing expensive products! There is no miracle drug to keep us young and we as Americans, are taught to be consumers of whatever we think will work. This is really a sad scenario as billions are wasted and the result is still the same. We all get old.

The following is not an exact quote from Mama, but very, very close. I can almost hear her voice saying:

"This growing old is the hardest thing I have ever done. You have to be tough. Growing old is a humbling experience. Imagine yourself the lovely young woman you are. Time passes by and you find yourself old. It happens just that quickly."

"Be prepared. One moment you are young, and the next moment you are old, and people look at you like you have done something wrong! Believe me, people do not look at you or treat you the same. This society just does not care about the elderly like other cultures."

"Please have empathy, compassion, and love for your elders, for soon you will turn into them. Once, not so long ago, I was young and full of health and energy. I think I was even pretty. I used to wonder what the old saying 'beauty comes from within' meant. Now I pray every day it is true as it sure as hell is not on the outside. My little shell of a body shows plenty of hard years, yet sometimes I feel inside my head, exactly as I did when I was young."

"Sometimes I get up in the morning and look in the mirror and feel like throwing up I wonder why in the world I have been able to live this long, and now what is my motivation. Then one of my children calls on the telephone and says 'I love you mama' and the thought leaves my head for the moment."

"Life is a funny thing. You spend half of it taking care of someone else, a husband, children, or people at work. Then when it is time for someone to return the favor, everyone seems to disappear like snow on a sunny day. Old people can be scary for sure. No one has time for old people. It is almost as if being old is a disease you have, and no one wants to be near those folks that have it."

"When you begin to age careers end and children leave. Money is tight, bodies change, youth disregards you, and most of your friends die."

"These changes can send you right into what I call a blue funk. I think undiagnosed depression has a grip on many old people."

"I understand that sometimes the needs of a young family is almost overwhelming. The need now for both parents to work just to survive has really changed the family unit."

"Elders are shuffled to a distant corner of everyone's life. Noone wants to be around someone who is slow in moving around and full of aches and pains."

"Once families all lived together and worked together. It is the industrialization of man that has dealt a fatal blow to many families, and in many ways began the ruination of man. It is a shame. It is a real loss for us all. No one wants to be reminded of his or her own mortality. Sometimes when I go to the store I find people have the need to patronize older people."

"I do not know why they just cannot understand all we need is a little kindness, a little affection, a little love."

"Sometimes people look right through you like you are invisible. It makes me so sad. All we want is to enjoy the company of someone younger occasionally. We can enjoy their youth vicariously. We wanted to be treated as equals and not inferiors simply because we are old."

"Once we were in the center of life. Once we were an authority of many things, we were not ignored and left alone for days at a time. Now I have noticed that hardly anyone is willing to listen to our problems, infirmities, and our fear of dying. People listen briskly and are briskly sympathetic. I will say it again, growing old is tough, and I am one of the lucky ones."

"I have you to help me baby. You will never know how much I appreciate all you do for me, and how sorry I am that I take up so much of your valuable time. You have made my last years exceptional because of your love for me."

"People can be very quick to criticize. It is so easy to pick out something to admire rather than pick out something to criticize. Try always to find the good in people and draw that out rather than pronounce their bad traits and make a big deal of that."

Mama was basically an optimist. I am grateful for that as a life full of aches and pains tends to make one cranky. I do thoroughly understand that. I am recovering from an accident and a very serious spinal cord injury. My thoughts often gravitate towards the immense pain Mama must have felt. I realize I never gave her enough accolades for bearing up under such trauma, mostly with smiles, and perhaps a bit of bitching once in a while.

I do remember one day I was so disgruntled by the negative energy and words she spouted at me, I immediately went home and wrote them down verbatim. This look from the inside of an elderly and disabled person is enlightening. I know from that day forward it as my job to try to turn these thoughts around some way, if I could.

"This is a death dance. I do not understand why I cannot be put to sleep mercifully like I did for my dogs when they were in horrible pain and too disabled to do anything. I have no dreams of the future; only fear of becoming more entrenched in pain and more disabled, and then losing my mind on top of it."

"I cannot drive, shop alone, sew, cook, paint or have sex. I cannot do anything. My eyes are so bad it is hard to read, and I do not have enough money to pay for new glasses or to get my teeth fixed. You pay into social security all your working life, and then the first things to go aren't even covered by insurance. It is not fair."

"I am not much use to anyone, not even myself. I have become a burden and a big mess. It is past time. I do not want to be here anymore. I feel so alone most of the time, and Daddy has been gone for years. I have nothing to look forward to except more wrinkles and more pain."

"I am constantly in pain, even with the morphine. It helps me but it also makes me sleepy, stupid and more constipated. My back, my hands, my feet, my knees, my God I do not understand what I did that was so bad I deserve to suffer like this. All I do is sit. I am totally bored and lonely."

"I cannot fall asleep at night, and there is no position to turn to that doesn't render pain. When I do finally sleep[, I have terrible dreams. I wake up each morning in pain and can hardly move. I have lost my taste for food, and almost everything on television is violence, rape and commercials for products to help you stay youthful."

"I can only sit and think about all the things I will never be able to do again in this lifetime. I do not believe this is happening to me. I do not want to lie. I want to die. I have read a book called Final Exit and know of many ways to do it."

"Bless Jack Kevorkian. Those people he helped die were suffering and they wanted to die. He was merciful to them by helping. The truth is I cannot kill myself because it would be a very poor example for my children and grandchildren. I need to show them courage and keep my faith in God and His laws. I am trapped alone with my overwhelming pain."

When I reread Mama's words I could not help but cry. I began to understand where she was coming from in a deeper way. I thank God she showed no hesitation in letting it all out or I might never have known some of these thoughts.

An old Cherokee adage says we need to step into another man's moccasins before we begin to judge them. Now that I am in Mama's moccasins, so to speak, my understanding has broadened even more in scope.

She was not just old and cranky. She had plenty of reasons to be cranky. It is your job, as a caregiver, to help turn thoughts of the elderly person you are caring for around.

You must help turn the negative to a positive so that the death dance cannot take hold. You can make lives be happier and more peaceful. It can be done. Whatever it takes, you must find a way.

I speak of mama throughout the book, but your "charge" may be your father, or grandfather. In such cases most hints are applicable but keep in mind, as men age PRIDE jumps right in the middle of the highway and screams- "No, this can't be happening."

This is a very touchy new challenge that enters the program.

R.W. Walker - Husband of 45 years,

wildcat oil driller, proud father of twins and

one daughter. He loved his family.

Daddy wrote these words to mama on their first anniversary. They were to have forty-four more years of sharing life's battles and joys together.

"With faith, with God, with compassion and understanding, with trust and soul and heart life can be like this, and it is!"

"The reward becomes a lifetime of happiness on a level unimagined in common hours."

"Suddenly you are complete. You are one with your wife and you feel a happiness that flows from being able to give of yourself to another, and knowing for certain that at last, finally, you belong together and will through all eternity."

"My love for you flourishes and deepens with every moment we share. You are the most wonderful thing in my entire world. You are my world."

Today so many people believe such amazing relationships are impossible. I just want to amend this chapter and add proof that with work and love, couples can enjoy a lifetime together.

I am privileged to know quite a few couples who have been married for decades. Mike and I are thirty-five years married.

This photo is of my cousin Roy, and his beautiful bride of fifty-seven years.

With God, work, and lots of love – this kind of joy is very possible for others.

Chapter 4

Chapter 4

How to Fill the Cup

It may be a challenge trying to change your aging mama's negative perspectives on life. Though Mama had been positive most of her life, we both found her getting more and more negative as the joys of life were slowly changing to increasing aches and pains.

She said there were few things she could look forward to, with the exception of more pain and less mobility.

I knew something had to be done. I prayed. I prayed and prayed and then prayed again. Ultimately, when I let go and let God take the reins the ideas started coming.

Early in those years of caring for Mama she was still able to move about fairly well. At that point I encouraged her to join a social club, go to the senior center, or find some friends in the apartment complex she lived in to play cards or shop together. She scoffed at my ideas, saying first she had too little money to run around, and then no money to dress nice enough. It was true.

The attorney who took Mama's malpractice case against the physician who killed my daddy, did everything he could to stretch the case out in length, and by the time she actually won, there was little money left for her.

She just wanted the doctor out of business so he wouldn't kill anyone else by mistake. His license was taken away, but sadly he just moved to Canada and began another practice.

Daddy had been working in Norway as an oilfield consultant. When he had bleeding, he was rushed home. The doctor did two exploratory surgeries, and then while daddy was drugged, the doctor had him sign for the third surgery.

It was the surgery that would ultimately

cause his death.

Mama never did get any of daddy's personal effects from the company he worked for prior to the surgeries. He had told her he had insurance papers and bank accounts in Oslo, Norway.

We never had the money to pursue getting the personal effects, so mama was left with just Medicare, and Social Security.

The budget was tight it was true, but I thought she always looked adorable and thought she was just making excuses because of shyness. After daddy died mama kind of retreated into a world of just family. All she wanted was family.

I made another suggestion. Why not sign up for community college classes? She liked that idea but only if I went with her. I understood why. At seventy-four years old it took a lot of courage to consider enrolling in school again. But she did it and for a few semesters she really enjoyed meeting people and learning new things.

Within weeks we learned mama needed a hip replacement and at the same time was diagnosed with osteoporosis and severe osteoarthritis. Her mobility began to diminish rapidly.

Whenever I was out of town, I made sure I kept a daily diary and took lots of photos. Upon returning I would hand the diary to mama. She would "take the trip with me" by reading the diary and looking at the photos. She felt more a part of the action outside her ever -shrinking world.

Her trips were limited to an occasional trip to the store, the post office, my house, or to the doctor's offices. There was not much to anticipate. As her osteoporosis took hold, her strength began to diminish, and she could not sit for long periods of time. Nor could she stand for long.

The only time she was comfortable was when she was lying down on her bed. She fought to keep the tears back as she said, "I just can't do it honey. My back is too weak and it hurts too much." My heart broke for Mama.

At least three or four times a week I would pick up a few new video releases and current events magazines. It helped Mama stay current with movies and events, and gave her great conversation material when she went to her weekly gab session at the beauty salon.

The salon day was a day to anticipate. All the women welcomed her and were very loving. It was a good change to be able to leave her small world and become a part of life again.

I must mention the kindness of one very special lady at that hair salon. Her name was Dorthea, and until Mama passed away this little angel would not take a penny when Mama came in to "get her hair done."

She fixed her hair each week and never charged her for it. On special days like Mama's birthday, she would cut or perm her hair, always free of charge.

Dorthea's kindness reminded me that there still are really such wonderful people on this planet; no matter what horrors the newscasts report daily.

I give Mama accolades for so many things. She opted to live alone as long as possible and absolutely refused to move in with my husband and me. "Nobody needs a mother-in-law living with them" she used to say, "that is ridiculous."

She tried to keep as physically fit as possible.

It is not easy when your body is racked with pain and it hurts simply to move. My background as a personal trainer came in handy more than once.

It is very important to try to make sure your mama drinks water and eats more than junk food. Food is the second most powerful natural substance you will ever put into your body, and your mama needs the right foods now more than ever. The wrong foods can add to her list of problems. They can make her age rapidly and even kill her prematurely.

Research has proven that the right foods can be one of the most powerful weapons in the battle against old age.

My friend, Jack LaLanne, also known as American's first fitness superhero, always said, "If man made it don't eat it."

Food CAN protect from degenerative illnesses like heart disease, cancer, diabetes, chronic fatigue arthritis, and osteoporosis. This list is just a partial list of illnesses that can be helped by proper nutrition. Foods can actually help neutralize damage done to a person's health in the past. Cells in the body can actually reverse in age.

This does not mean your mama will stop aging, but preventative good nutrition will help her maintain the best health possible throughout these last, most difficult years.

I truly believe my mama was so sharp mentally because of her consistency in eating a very healthy diet throughout most of her life. That does not mean she did not fall off the nutrition wagon once in a while.

What hurt her the most I believe, like many seniors affected, is that there is a point Mama said, "It's no fun cooking for just me. I am not up to cooking or shopping. Truly I am not much interested in eating. I am sick of everything."

Many seniors have been diagnosed with dehydration and anorexia; even my beloved mama once.

We are human machines that need oxygen, water and food. Without them, we die. Because this is so important, I will expand the vision of your parent and a lack of water and food. We can only live for several weeks without food, several days without water, and minutes without oxygen. We are a volatile and precision mechanism.

You have seen those sad and horrible television advertisements regarding starving children in many countries. Your heart probably breaks for them, as does mine. Can you picture your mama with her rib case protruding from her chest? Can you picture her cheeks sunken and her skeleton showing outside her entire body?

Can you imagine the mechanics of her body starving and also without water? When one vital organ does not receive the quota of water it needs every day those organs will automatically begin to steal water from other organs within your body. If you cannot imagine that, then look at one of your houseplants. If it does not get enough good soil and water, it dies! Got the picture?

Because we do these things (breathing, drinking, and eating) pretty much without thought, we rarely think of the fact vital organs, bones, intestines, vision, hearing, even thought processes respond to how we treat our bodies.

DO NOT be naïve. Recently I was appalled to read an article that said about sixty percent of our seniors suffer from problems I just mentioned. It is almost impossible to believe that these problems are on the increase and not the decline. These facts have been well established.

Now focus in on the ten thousand people who are turning sixty-five every single day. We have a problem!

It is difficult to monitor these things, and especially if you live in a separate area than that of your mama. We must help our aging population. If you notice that your mama seems to have a dwindling appetite, start cooking.

She will eat just because of the effort you have made. Make sure you have an extra bottle of water with you when you take her places with you.

Begin to enforce good nutritional habits for her. She did it for you when you were young. Even if she didn't do that, please try to start changing the world by changing the lives of one parent at a time.

A way to help build good habits regarding all of these critical body functions, is to keep reminding her of the importance of the healing properties available through foods and water.

When I cooked for my own family, I usually made enough to take dinners to Mama.

She loved it, and proved that she still had an appetite by eating every bite. We had her over to join us for supper – but not often enough.

A way to neutralize depression is by getting the body to produce more of its own "feel good" chemicals (called endorphins). These chemicals occur naturally as you begin to exercise. Once the brain starts producing more of these endorphins, your neurotransmitters will improve your mood. This will work for your mama too. Even moderate exercise helps. Exercise is the way to call upon the body's natural antidepressants.

It is one of the reasons why people who make exercise a habit, really hesitate to quit. This exercise high is not in the imagination; it is the actual physiological change in the human body.

Try to encourage exercise of some sort when you can, even it is just sitting in a chair and stretching fingers and wiggling toes. All movement keeps the elderly **ABLE** to move. Inactivity breeds stiffness and keeps oxygen from moving throughout the body.

Lack of movement keeps injuries from healing as quickly. It also causes constipation. I know this is unpleasant to talk about, but it is very important to discuss so your mama will stay as healthy as possible.

It is also a fact, many people do not know, that when we do not get enough water to our internal organs begin to take the water from one another. Water is second only in importance to oxygen. I wish I had known more about different methods to help Mama at the time.

Many of the prescriptions our seniors take cause severe constipation. In order to keep the body functioning optimally, remember that constipation is actually our sewer system backing up, causing "dis-ease, and disease". I remember Mama rubbing her tummy and saying, "Oh I wish I could go to the bathroom." Encourage hydrating as most seniors do not drink enough water.

There is another way to help cleanse the body, but our medical professionals mostly do not acknowledge it as something that is acceptable. They either say they know nothing about Colon Hydro Therapy, or that it is not something they can write a prescription to help with the cost. Possibly that kind of response originated in the fact the physicians cannot receive a financial windfall from a pharmaceutical company for prescribing a colonic.

Colonics are not new. They have been around for at least thirty-seven hundred years, and are an important part of homeopathic healing programs. Just like many Chinese therapies, the medical profession refuses to acknowledge the validity of hydro therapy/irrigation.

After I had a spinal cord injury and major surgeries, my colon did not function normally because of nerve damage. I located a reputable Certified Colon Hydro Therapist and began weekly therapy.

Because my colon has severe nerve root injuries, and because of the strong medications I must take for the pain, I am unable at all to have a normal bowel movement regularly. I would prefer not to mention this however, it may help you to feel more at ease about the subject.

It is urgent to care for your colon! More people than we realize have similar problems. Were it not for the expert care this Certified Colon Hydro Therapist gives me weekly, I would really be in life-threatening trouble physically without the help.

At my first appointment, I was ready to check in, and an elderly lady said to me, "Oh my, I have had pain in my back and stomach for a year and no doctor was able to help me. This lovely woman has saved my life. She was sent from God." I concur.

Your colon transports waste material to exit your body. If you think about it, this function is urgent in keeping the body fit. No exercise in the world matters if your colon is not working!

Wherever you are located you will probably be able to find a colon therapist near enough to help.

Mama was pretty good at keeping herself as busy as possible. She used to say, "Busy hands are happy hands." One afternoon, early on before she was seriously inhibited from movement, she painted her little back porch turquoise! Then she dropped a little glitter all around and spread little turquoise rocks throughout the dirt in her little yard. It looked great and really brightened up the place.

When Mama was a few years younger, she used to take painting classes, and love them. I began hitting all the thrift stores in the area to buy whatever little sculptures I could find. I took her to a craft store and she got all the paint and miscellaneous things she would need to work on the sculptures.

The first time I brought a little boy sculpture to her I said, "He is adorable, but he needs to be painted to give him new life." She loved the idea of giving the sculptures a new life. Her mission became to revitalize these sculptures.

I purchased any sculpture or small people I could find. Mama anticipated working on them, but was at a loss of what to do with them when she finished each one.

I suggested she give some of them to family and friends as gifts. She signed and dated the bottom or back of each one. I thought that might be a good way to give her a way to gifts, and also give each family member something to treasure when she passed on.

Many of the things looked brand new when she finished them, and at one point I found myself taking many of them home to enjoy. For the others I found boxes and wrapping and she had a second goal.

Get them ready for birthdays, Christmas, or simply gifts of love. As the old saying goes, she really did have a new lease on life.

Every time she finished a job I could tell. She beamed and showed the completed item to me saying, "Do you like it? Is it okay to share?" She was always proud to accomplish finishing each one. It is important for your mama to feel as if she is still doing something productive in this life.

At eighty-two years old, with arthritic little fingers that pointed in every direction, and eyes that saw less clearly each day, she had become quite the artist. She appreciated having something to do that was fun.

She said every senior needs a hobby they can do it with a passion. It changed so many lonely and boring hours for her to productive and pleasurable hours.

When Mama passed, I was able to share something hand-painted with all those in the family, and her many friends.

Many seniors have limited physical prowess and their world grows smaller by the day.

She told me one time that she had no dreams and no future. Give your mama something to make her happy to be alive! Whether it be painting, knitting, sewing, cooking, writing, or whatever, encourage her to be productive in her areas of interest. Praise her for her efforts. Even if perfection is not met, give her accolades for the efforts.

I personally did more praying than I do on a regular basis. One of the things that troubles young people about older people is they see them as out of step with what is happening today

Bring books, magazines, DVDs, newspapers, practically anything that is current.

It will keep your mama well informed. It will also keep your mama's intellect and memory sharp.

The technology of today is just the beginning of a new world. I do not necessarily think it is a better world, but there are some real benefits for seniors if they learn the basics. Many cities and towns have classes to teach seniors this technology.

You may check with the colleges, the library, and for heaven's sake, check on the Internet. A great thing about the information highway is there is HELP out there if you just do a bit of research.

Listen to your mama. Really listen. I remember for weeks every time I would go to visit Mama, she would start talking about politics. I was delighted she was so informed but politics to me were just not that interesting. As an individual I am a political atheist.

I think the majority of them are career politicians, and most I have learned over a lifetime, most are liars. God help the American people.

Since politics was not of high interest to me, I really got antsy and impatient when she would go on and on about how she could not stand Bill Clinton. She kept a file of all the negative media reports about him. She would have been interested in learning all that happened to him since her death. But getting back to the point, politics was of high interest to her.

Her life was limited and I should have just really listened and respected her knowledge and savvy conversations. It really would not have been that painful, and you never know, you might learn something new while listening.

One day I thought I was filled to the brim and could not handle any more. I got a pad and notepaper, and I told her I wanted to hear things about her and her experiences that no one else had ever heard. Hear about her life.

I told her I was writing a story about her (and I actually am in the process of completing that soon). When she got tucked away her insecurities about writing, she began to relax and her stories were really fascinating. I heard incredible things I would NEVER have known if I had not taken the time to ASK and LISTEN.

I opened a treasure chest of history and it was fantastic!

Your aging mama may feel at times disgusted with her own face and body, tired, full of pain, and she may feel just worthless. For the majority of seniors this WILL happen. This is really true for someone who has depended on her looks and body for her success. Aging will be traumatic.

Please be careful of words that come from your mouth. Words can tear her down even further, and trust me on this, they will come back to haunt you. Mama always felt true beauty comes from the heart, and even so, she worried about the visual aspects of the aging process.

Treat your mama like a real friend. Once Mama told me that she was so happy I talked to her like a friend, and that I did not patronize her (role reversal). She said in doing so I also kept her vocabulary current, which she said made people treat her like she was younger. This culture is truly obsessed by youth and beauty.

She gave me insight that as people grow older, they often become shy in expressing feelings. She thought it was because so often people seem disinterested in hearing what older people have to say.

"Just because our exterior is old" she would say, "It does not mean our ideas or thoughts are old too. We just need the chance to be involved and join back in the mainstream of life." As time I certainly do understand what she meant.

Occasionally I would try to do something with Mama that was totally different. I tried to create for her a change of pace. She often told me she had cabin fever and wished she could be free to drive alone again.

Her osteoporosis had gotten so bad she had lost several inches in height. She had to put several pillows on the car seat to just see out the window. I really thought it would be safer for me to drive and easier for her, most of the time.

I took her to art shows, Native American gatherings with lots of crafts and artwork, to watch the salmon run,
antique shops, and even to a gun show. She loved it all.

Once I told Mama to grab her hat and get in my vehicle. It was the fourth of July. I took off the T-top and drove back and forth on a short stretch of freeway, where the city fireworks were going off, and it was practically overhead.

She said the view was perfect and the wind and excitement were exhilarating. I was so happy I had chosen to take her on that particular adventure.

One of the best ideas, inspired by God I am certain, was to take her a gift of a book to write in, and a cassette tape recorder for her to use. She asked "What am I supposed to write? I am no writer and my life is boring. What do I do with the tape recorder?"

I suggested she share her years of wisdom with the family. Perhaps, I suggested, she could write a book about what were the most important things to her in life, or things that would help the younger children as they met stumbling blocks in their lives.

The book would become a part of their heritage to her children and grandchildren.

As far as the tape was concerned, I suggested it might be a good idea for her to express her last thoughts to her family, and her wishes concerning her death, when the time arrived. So many people hesitate to talk about death to the older generation.

Mama needed to talk about it. She needed to share her fears and concerns. She brought it up to me. In the beginning I refused to talk about it at all. But it was one of the most thoughtful things she could have done for me in the long run. *The subject of death needs companionship.*

She assured me that death is as natural as being born, and though sometimes people are afraid of it, ultimately, we all have to die. Death is part of being alive and even if we don't understand why we must die, it will happen to us all.

We talked for hours about spiritual things, about the afterlife, and what she wanted to do regarding her funeral and burial. It helped her to handle thoughts that were already crowding in her mind.

Wisely she also took me around her apartment showing me things that she wanted to leave with specific people. Doing so made her feel as if things were more settled.

We sat one afternoon and delved into her personal papers and her will. A few days earlier she insisted we get a durable power of attorney for health care. She had specific wishes about her last days and she wanted me to be able to follow her wishes. It eased her mind for me to know all the details. She felt better knowing business was complete for her death arrangements and wishes.

Mama was so burdened with severe osteoporosis. At the time our medical society did not pay too much attention to the needs of women. I had to research osteoporosis by going online and also calling different universities and medical facilities.

I was honest with her about my findings, and I was sure to ask questions when we were at her doctor appointments! I believe God gave me the words to be honest and yet not put her in a position of giving up all hope.

Always leave the subject of illness and disabilities on a positive note, if possible.

Research has been comprehensive and today the startling statistics are that one of two women will get osteoporosis, and one of four men. It is a very serious problem.

The elderly face the reality of death around the next corner they turn.

We all need hope. Hope liberates us from the chains of disability and pain. Pray if you believe in the power of prayer, and if you do not, you might try praying anyway! It certainly cannot hurt.

We even talked about giving her a way out of this life if she ever got really bad, and felt she could not face another day. We went as far as to smash up some of her sleeping pills and morphine to make what she called her "death pill". She never used it.

Ultimately what we discovered when she had a heart attack, was that the survival instinct kicked in. She still wanted to live. She finally told me again, "I cannot kill myself."

"I cannot take the chicken way out. I must be a good example for my family, and show them I can be courageous no matter what."

I was quite relieved of course as during the time before this discussion she begged me to just put a bag over her head and hold it there until she was gone. I adamantly said, NO! NO! NO! She just really needed to get these thoughts out in the open and review the future with someone.

Be kind to your mama, and patient. It takes great effort to walk slower. It takes extra strength to lift wheelchairs and have extra weight leaning on you for support. It is difficult to give up freedom and add more work to the schedule of an already full plate.

This care giving is no easy task.

It will take a toll on you if you let it. Nonetheless, if you practice thinking of positive solutions, and keep your thoughts loving, you can change the impossible to possible. It can be done. Eventually, with God's help, I did it.

Exercise your ability to treat your mama as a very important person. Treat her with respect and dignity, and do not belittle her because she is old and unable to care for herself. Mama wanted freedom. She did not want any person to have to commit time to help her. She felt terrible, at times, for taking up so much of my time. I was honored, and even more so when she passed.

Have fun with your mama.

There is nothing more healing that laughter and hugs between family and friends. It is a proven fact that hugs and kisses are important. When mama turned eighty years old, she told me she really appreciated the affection I showed her.

She stressed out to the max when she looked in the mirror. She said she felt old and wrinkled, and wondered why any- one would want to kiss her.

This may sound farfetched, but our elderly have too much time on their hands to think and become critical of themselves.

This care giving is the greatest challenge you will ever face. I once told her that turnabout was fair play.

I remember falling asleep as a child with a kiss and a whisper of "I love you" softly in my ear. Do not let their free time become a nightmare dealing with their fears and pain.

I always held Mama's hand and she just loved it. It also gave me the confidence to know if she tripped or lost her footing, I was right there to help her.

God works His miracles in wondrous ways for sure.

I found Mama a large print Bible so she could read it easier, and I ordered her a subscription of the Daily Word. She read it each morning and I think it would apply in some way, to her situation, and instantly it made her feel better.

Guidepost is another magazine that packs a wallop of good things in its pages. Most magazines can be ordered with large print. I often rented movies for her to watch. Many libraries will have shelves of movies and informative DVD's or CD's that are free to use.

When your mama is cranky, depressed, or negative, remember how you would like to be treated if roles were reversed.

Sometimes seniors are cranky because they are dealing with lots of pain.

Change yourself with positive thoughts. It will take practice but positive thoughts culminate in positive results, and if you stay positive, it will help you and your mama.

No matter what our disadvantage or problem, our handicap, is our response; if it is sour and negative that will set the tone of any scenario.

Bring her flowers from your garden. Pick up an extra artichoke or candy bar at the store for her.

Surprise her. One of the things I did for

Mama that she liked best was put together

for her, an earthquake readiness backpack.

It contained water, a light warm blanket, a

flashlight, dried fruit, a first aid kit, and a

few other items. She was thrilled. She said it

made her feel a part of the living community,

and also let her know she was worth saving!

Sometimes the smallest things you do for

your mama will make the biggest difference

in her happiness. To develop her zest for

living again we must see through our hearts

and have great understanding.

Remind your mama we are like unfinished works of art, and each thought we think, each movement we make, and each task we complete, adds another stroke to the canvas. Encourage her positive emotions by applauding her capability to handle such challenges (even if she had been behaving badly recently).

Commend her and draw out her wonderful self by being a wonderful person to her.

Soon your job of care giving will finish and you will never have another opportunity to do anything for your mama again.

Consider you have the task of fulfilling her last days with loving concern and fun. You will grow and gain in wisdom beyond your wildest dreams. You will give yourself the gift of knowing what to expect as your age and step into her shoes. I am there, and I am grateful for the knowledge she imparted to me. It makes my growing older, just that much more manageable. It has made me stronger and more accepting.

If you can manage to meet with members of your family that may participate in her care, or even contact them via email or snail mail, it will be advantageous for all concerned for you to share your ideas and thoughts.

Just something as simple as reaching in her mailbox and finding a note from a loved one would make her grin all day.

The note need not be for a holiday, perhaps just a quick love message to say hi.

She always loved receiving pictures drawn by the younger members of the family. She would proudly display them on her refrigerator.

Take a breath and say a prayer. Do these things often as they will help you and the person whom you are giving your time and energy.

"Give, and it shall be given unto you; good measure, pressed down, and shaken together, and running over, shall men give into your bosom. For with the same measure that ye mete withal it shall be measured to you again."

Luke 6:38

"But the fruit of the Spirit is love, joy, peace, longsuffering, gentleness, goodness, faith, Meekness, temperance: against such there is no law."

Galatians 5:22-23

"Honor widows that are widows indeed. But if any widow has children or nephews let them first shew piety at home, and to requite their parents, for that is good and acceptable before God."

1 Timothy 5:3-4

Chapter 5

Chapter 5

What if She's Bossy, whiney and Rude?

She said, "I wonder if it would have been easier to lose my mind than the use of my body. I would not know then how bad things were".

As I sat across the dining room table from

mama, I noticed the arthritic deformities on Mama's knuckles had grown larger.

Her complexion was pink and her skin looked soft. She was always careful to look well-groomed and clean. She caught me staring at her face and said, "I know why you are looking at me that way."

She had a smile on her face. "It is the look that always says you are loving me!" She was right. How could I not?

She tried so hard to be happy most of the time, regardless of her pain and trials. I would give anything were I able to glance across the table to give her that look. But that time has passed, and though it may be difficult, you must make the time you have left, good for your mama.

Sooner than you think she will be gone. Or your father. Time speeds by and we forget to love the ones we love, more frequently.

All the bones in her hands were very large and deformed; a result of osteoarthritis. The osteoporosis had already caused Mama's spine to bend forward, and her height had dwindled to a mere four foot, six inches. She often called herself the incredible shrinking woman, and incredible she was!

I often kidded Mama that she was the only woman I knew who could point ten directions at one time. It really was not funny, but she knew I meant it to make light of her problem, and with a great sense of humor, she accepted it as such. She said it made her special.

Osteoarthritis and osteoporosis are painful and debilitating.

I know now that I am beginning to suffer from joints that are enlarged and painful, just how much it hurts. When I say painful, I mean you may be sitting quietly and suddenly you feel a jolt of pain that seems to have manifested from out of the clear blue sky! Painful stuff this arthritis.

The times we could make light and joke about the circumstances elevated both our dispositions. A sense of humor is invaluable when you are taking care of an elderly person.

I remember not fully understanding why some days she was so irritable and nasty. I could remember having pain and I handled it.

She was still mentally sharp and still able to live in her own space. I just thought it was the getting old and cranky syndrome you hear about so often. You know, the one that says that all old people are crabby and irritating. I have come to discover many older people have valid reasons to act thusly.

Pain can wear on you. Nagging pain that simply does not go away, but increases in small increments. It is mentally disabling. She once told me that when you get old it is not just one new pain a day, but always two or three. She was once again correct.

She never expounded to say often the pain was unbearable. I knew.

I remember a day mama was particularly irritable. I was barely clinging to a calm and happy feeling that day, but she just kept pulling me down with her constant complaining. One day I had reached my breaking point, and I gave it back to her. I asked just what in the hell was going on.

"Well," she said, "It was twelve years ago today that dad died. I never thought I would outlive him. He had such a yearning to live, and such a zest for life. But I am glad he did not have to deal with this aging thing. Sometimes the pain seems unreal."

"Life for me right now is kind of like giving someone a mansion to live in and then making them live in a tiny wooden box."

"I never thought I would be like this. I am unable to move much without staggering pain."

"When ten to twenty million women have osteoporosis, why have we not heard much about it before? I simply do not want anyone to see my crooked back. I look like the hunchback of Notre Dame."

"I do not want anyone to know how much pain I am in. If there was only hope of improving it would be easier, but it will only get worse. I am so discouraged and depressed. The only hopes I have are the promises God has given to us. I am MORE than ready to die."

Tears began to fill her eyes, almost hiding what a beautiful pale blue in color they were. They trickled down her cheeks and fell her chin. It makes me cry as I write this. No one can be blamed for fearing a job care giving an elderly parent or relative. It is painful to see those you love in such a state.

She was trying hard not to cry and I remember she told me when I was young, "Cry pretty honey". She was still pretty. From within her heart and through those eyes there was no aging of her Spirit wish I had not been snappy with her. I then understood the why of that mood that particular day.

Since Mama's death, I found, and continue to find, a deeper understanding of why the elderly are often unhappy. At best they face their own mortality, a loss of most freedoms, a deteriorating body, and quite often pain in the body that is horrific. No dreams, and often times, no one to love them.

That scenario is quite a challenge to face with a consistent happy face. Mama did a very good most of the time.

The elderly must face increasing pain, and the dread of being a burden to the ones they love. For those with no family a real fear of being the recipient of elder abuse in an honest concern.

This news was quite a surprise to me.

There are one and a quarter million young caregivers. These are the hidden caregivers because no one else is there to do it. What a responsibility for a young person. A favorite saying among many of these young caregivers is "When my grandma is happy, I am happy."

From me to young caregivers, I say, "God bless you and your recipients."

Remember dealing with an ordinary case of the blues is not something that cannot be handled, but lingering depression can be signs of other problems. If depression is severe and seems to be a lengthy problem, the time might be time to check into diet, and possibly refer to a doctor for professional help - although I believe God gives us intuition if we are still and listen.

On occasion we forget we do have the choice of how we handle what is placed before us. We may not be able to change what is happening, but we can, one hundred percent of the time, change our attitude and response to it.

Remind your mama how strong she is and that she still has control of many choices, and using her mind in many decisions. What can you do to help during those down days or in minor cases of depression? First, keep in mind there may be many of those days, and try to rehearse responses for different types of scenarios. Then remember you cannot possibly understand the depth of worry that facing these traumas may cause your mama. Do not expect to have instant patience, but TRY to be patient. Remember those words you speak will come back to haunt you after she is gone. They will permeate her heart while she is here, and add to her already growing doubts and concerns.

You do not want to do that!

Mama used to say, "I don't want any trouble." Our elderly citizens have plenty to handle dealing with each day.

PRAY, PRAY and then PRAY.

God does hear prayers, and though you might not think you are getting an answer, just keep praying. This is the time to show your faith by trusting.

Once when we were in a restaurant Mama was very rude to the waiter. Perhaps he was not the best waiter, but I knew if I let the continued outbreaks occur, our outings would be ruined.

I wanted each day to be one she could remember. I simply if she was going to be crabby like a lot of other old people, I could find better things to do than spend my time with her. Sometimes when people start on a downward spiral, the trend can become a habit, and often with no real reason motivate the bad behavior. This was one of those times.

I was not cross with her, just factual. She got the message and snapped right out of her mood. I actually think my honesty with her helped change her mood on more than one occasion. She liked being treated like a peer and a friend. She liked my honesty.

She often mentioned often older people feel like they are treated like they have no brains. "We may be slow," she said, "but most of us can still think."

There may be times it will be necessary to involve yourself in aspects of your mama's life that you would really rather not!

These are the times you must work to put aside your own feelings and remember the tedious duties most parents have done for his or her children during their childhood. Anyone who has ever had children knows exactly what I mean.

Children must be cleaned and sometimes the job is downright nasty. Whether they have runny noses or runny bowels, a child is cared for by whomever is in charge and that is as simple that. When you approach these kinds of tasks with your mama, be grateful she is grown up and help her as much as you can.

No one wants to have to ask for help, and particularly in personal tasks, but this little book gave birth in part, with the intention of helping, so these tasks must be discussed. Your parent may be unable to shower alone or even manage a sponge bath. You may need to clean up messes that involve the urine or bowel movements.

You may need to change bandages and clean areas that are dreadful to see. Do what you can to make these tasks easier and make your mama feel less like a terrible burden. She will feel like a burden if you take little care in how you present yourself when helping her.

My mama appreciated the help I gave her, and was relieved to be able to share some of her disability or hardships with someone else. The burdens of ailments and aging can be overwhelming. While you are at it, ask if she would like her back scratched, or her feet rubbed. As you give in this life, so shall you receive. Beyond expecting something in return, remember (even if she is too mortified to say it), how much she appreciates the help.

The staggering loss of freedom she feels by losing just the ability to do these personal tasks, can truly cause great depression. With great creativity you can help in more than simply physically accomplishing personal tasks.

Other jobs for you might include such simple things as tying her shoelaces, cutting her toenails or even brushing her hair. Try to enjoy the fact you are sharing time together and mention how soft her hair is, or give her a hand or shoulder massage. The small things you do will be monumental to her, and whatever you do will lighten your burden and heal both your hearts.

I was not thrilled about being involved in such things as incontinence and feminine problems. I think that it was because the facts I was learning put a little fear into the prospect of aging, myself. I felt like I was learning more than I actually wanted to know.

As a part of this position, you may learn things you would rather learn a few years "down the road" – not at present. Just accept it as cheerfully as you can. I am grateful now for knowing some things to expect and how to handle them for myself.

When you begin to care for a disabled or ill parent, you might feel as if you are on overload and ready to blow up. You may have extra shopping and cooking to do. You may find yourself pushing and lifting a wheelchair, carrying extra groceries, doing extra housework, etc!

You must keep in mind that as a caregiver these tasks will become second nature to you.

We women particularly do have the capacity to handle one hundred things at one time. God never gives us more than we can handle. Though honestly, it may seem so at times. You must keep your faith strong.

Mothers all over the world rise to the occasion of doing the impossible every single day after the birth of their child. We are familiar with stepping beyond even our own presumed limits and we are able to do it as a caregiver. In keeping your own sanity, and hers, you must be clever in creating moments of joy for you both to share.

I remember the first time I went grocery shopping for Mama.

She felt pretty good that day so I left the bags on the kitchen sink for her to put the things away. She said she wanted to do it. The next day I walked into her apartment and the first thing she said was "DON'T EVER BUY ME THAT KIND OF PAPER TOWELS AGAIN!"

I was stunned. Not only was I verbally reprimanded, but when I tried to make my escape. I reached for the door knob and saw a large piece of paper with a reminder in large black letters – Do not forget! Do not EVER buy those paper towels for me again. I was livid then. I already felt the burden of having to go to six different stores to get specific items.

I felt as if she had just slapped me right in the face. I thought Mama should have been glad I was there to shop, and had gone to all the different stores.

Here is what I did not know at the time. At least I did not think far enough into her realm to realize that she had spent years learning which items were the best, and also, finding the best bargains. She learned which products were quality items and which ones were not. She was careful to shop and purchase each item with forethought.

Shopping had become a friend in a way. How many times have you seen an older person alone in the grocery store?

It was a time she was out in the public. She read labels and checked out each item. She could visit with other shoppers and the cashiers. It was an EVENT.

Now she was totally unable to even shop. If I deemed her learned knowledge as if it were nothing, I would be taking away what was very nearly the only things now, she was in charge of, and the importance of her choices. I was somehow would be removing her worth as a person as well.

The revelation helped as I realized she needed to be in charge of something.

She needed to make decisions that were important.

Her knowledge was important and though it took a few minutes longer, I respected her and shopped as she had asked.

In the process I learned quite a bit about some pretty practical things. Have you ever heard of Fels-Naptha Soap? It is a bar of heavy laundry soap that is reasonable and will remove practically any stain, whether old or new. It is a great value. I learned about it by shopping to buy the products Mama specifically requested.

I thank God many lessons were learned before I lost mama. However sometimes wisdom is slow in arriving, and even today I think of things I could have improved upon.

It is when we feel deep regret we must try to accept that this whole career of "care giving" (unless you are a professional) is unmapped.

Mama's life was very limited. She wrestled with her life having meaning and value at that particular late stage in years. As I mentioned earlier, you may have to help your mama with things of a much more personal nature. There may be many times you just have to wing your response to her need. Say a prayer and take a breath.

You will find in caring for her you will not only be her adult child, you will become her most personal friend, and confidant.

In making your mama happy these last years, you will in turn be offered much in your own future success. In retrospect the education I gained was a big help in easing for me into the jolt of aging. Knowledge is power when applied. When you are aware of impending changes in your life, often your responses will be more thoughtful and even wiser.

If you feel awkward initially, just remember how it may be embarrassing for your mama. She has been an independent adult for more years than you can remember. Think of how humbling and humiliating it may be for her to have needs now she cannot fulfill alone. My mama found it difficult to turn over her power to someone else.

I think, however, what bothered Mama the most, was her body.   She was ashamed that she was so wrinkly and old. She kept saying, "I have never had a tummy until a few years ago. Now I cannot get rid of it. I wish my skin were not so thin and fragile. Every time I touch something I get a big black and blue mark. I am so bent over with osteoporosis I look squashed like a little bug just stepped on!"

I thought, WHAT HAVE WE DONE TO OUR ELDERLY that someone as wonderful as my Mama could feel so ashamed?

My answer - we have placed so much importance on the flaw-less exterior of youthful faces and bodies that we have forgotten to value and treasure the heart from within a person.

Consumerism has become our national pastime, and every commercial and advertisement places the most value on what a person looks like on the outside.

Fake everything. Skin is airbrushed, breasts are augmented, behinds are shaped, and facelifts and Botox injections are in demand. I cannot imagine injection snake venom into my face in order to take some wrinkles away. Wrinkles are inevitable. You can count on wrinkles with the same certainty you can count on death. They come to us all whether we like it or not.

There is no other country in the world that treats their elders as shabbily as we do. We are blessed to be residing in the greatest country of all and yet our elders have become throwaways.

Remember when you are fighting exhaustion, a lack of time, and you feel like you cannot go on, your mama is fighting just to go on. She is fighting for her life.

The position of caregiver is not forever and when it is over, so is the earthly relationship you share with your mama. Keep this in mind as these moments pass quickly.

You will suddenly find yourself making arrangement to say goodbye for the last time. Your sorrow will be multiplied if you have not taken care of business lovingly.

Forgive quickly and never doubt the capacity you have as a woman or a man to do the impossible. God is our light and He is always shining for us. When we are at our weakest, He is at his strongest. You may have forgotten to pray your fears and uncertainty to Him, but if you feel depleted find a quiet place and pray.

If you are an agnostic or atheist, even just moments of meditation and breathing will readily help you to regain strength and confidence.

This is probably not the career you imagined, but necessary to help and love EITHER parent.

The care for an aging male will be somewhat different, but the bottom line is love, flexibility, and dependability!

"This is my commandment, that ye love one another as I have loved you. Greater love has no man than this, than a man lay down his life for his friends."
John 15:12-13

"Hearken unto thy father that begat thee, and despise not thy mother when she is old."
Proverbs 23: 22

"Fear thou not; for I am with thee: be not dismayed; for I am thy God; I will strengthen thee; yea, I will help thee; ye, I will uphold thee with the right hand of my righteousness."

Isaiah 41:10

"... If ye have faith as a grain of mustard seed, ye shall say unto this mountain, remove hence, to yonder place and it shall move; and nothing shall be impossible unto you."

Matthew 17:20

Chapter 6

Chapter 6
A Reason to Live

This chapter is simply to remind you of one of the most important things you can do for your aging mama. GIVE HER A REASON TO LIVE!

There were so many days when Mama said, "Your love for me gives me a reason to live. It gives me a reason to be alive.

Sometimes when I wake up it is so hard to even get out of bed, but knowing that you need me to be here is reason enough to keep on trying."

Women particularly NEED a reason to live. We are creatures who seem to function better when we are accomplishing some-thing. We need a purpose in life. As an older woman, the tasks of a lifetime seem to vanish into thin air. The need to be needed grows more intense, while the truth of the matter is the elderly are "needed" less and less in today's reality.

It seemed when Mama was working towards a goal she temporarily forgot about her wrinkles and her bending little spine.

Her pain even seemed to diminish. When she was working towards a goal she was inspired. It did not matter what the task, there was a reason to live.

When she was able, Mama used to make it her business to cook a meal to share with us. She cooked at least a couple of times a week. Sometimes she just cut up a big salad and gave it to me to take home for supper.

I always gave her accolades for her work and told her how much I appreciated the thoughtfulness. I knew her arthritic fingers must have hurt after all that chopping. What I should have done more often was insist I take her home to have supper with us when she was able.

Even if it meant an extra trip to return her to her apartment, I should have been more thoughtful in this instance. Hindsight is 20/20 but often sadder than you would like it to be.

I know now her fingers must have been extremely painful and I am only dealing with a bit of arthritis in one finger!

Sometimes the work I did for Mama felt like busy work to me. I thought she wanted to keep me with her longer and that probably was true on many occasions.

A lovely result of some of the work she did that I had dreamed up for her, was that she was clever in her repairs and work, and the end product usually turned out to be great. She was a clever little woman. She just needed inspiration.

I asked Mama one time to make a list of the things she considered most important in her life, and this is what she wrote to me:

"The most important things in my life are a faith that truly sustains me, a friend who stands by me no matter what, a clear conscience, a family that loves me, a hobby that consumes me, good judgment, consideration of my fellow man, and an appreciation for all the living animals and birds, and the earth itself."

Wow! That was to me, an unexpected, and wonderful consolidation of her thoughts.

It also contained several clues that I could have used to help mama, and give her those special reasons to live.

Perhaps she needed a large letter Bible for pleasure and study, or a regular time to read and pray together would have helped to fulfill her days. I bought several magazines with photos of lots of birds, and great books with different places in the world to see. It was kind of like being able to travel, if only visually.

I took my dog to visit her and she loved it particularly because she was unable to keep a pet for herself.

I contacted friends and family and reminded them Mama was unable to drive alone and she would appreciate them stopping by. I also took her to visit friends when I had the time.

Remember these are her FINAL years on the planet. With as many problems as our elderly must endure, we need to do our best to create the feeling that truly they are loved and wanted.

Be creative in your ideas for your mama, and don't be skimpy on spending time with her. I spent a lot of time with mama, but I know I could have done more. It would not have taken too much time to juggle my calendar. I know now that part of my not spending more time with her was just my own selfishness. Love requires sacrifice!

Three of the worst enemies for the elderly are loneliness, boredom, and the feeling that they are not needed in this world any more.

Most seniors can deal with the pains and various aches (with a little positive feedback and medical help), but the other enemies can destroy faster than any physical disability. Enlist the entire family!

My daughter loved her grandma and was delighted when she got time from school and work, to be with her. She always hugged her grandma, and kissed her right on the lips.

My husband was wonderful too, and always held hands with her, and went the extra mile to make sure her car was running and in great mechanical shape.

His work was so appreciated, and it saved her part of the precious little money she had to exist on.

I remember after he worked on her vehicle, she would tell me, "We need to take the car to get it washed. It runs better if it is clean."

I know it sounds silly, but I swear it ran better immediately after we had it washed. It may have had something to do with the work my husband had lovingly just finished, but I never mentioned that.

I hope your mama will be one of the fortunate seniors who have to only endure the normal effects of aging.

If she is burdened with emergency after emergency, and trauma after trauma, realize this, it is the challenge of a lifetime for BOTH of you! Rise to meet her needs.

Fall to your knees to ask for help when you feel you cannot go on any longer. Though at the time you may not feel you can go further you can! Humans are made to endure, both physically and mentally. We regenerate and begin again...

Assure her that you are there for the long run and she will respond.

She may just need that assurance to go on herself, and you may need to say it more than once. In turn she will teach you more about life and yourself than you could ever imagine.

She will empower you with knowledge of the days to come for yourself, and help in the preparation to handle all the challenges of YOUR future, and with grace.

Your choices will be threads of golden opportunity to be woven into the tapestry of each day thereafter.

The things learned as a caregiver will enhance the days of your life, and will be shared with those in the circle of your life.

I think my Mama was exceptional (most of us like to think our families are the best) but some of the most fun Mama created for herself was games she devised using her own imagination.

One game she played was with the many teddy bears, stuffed animals and dolls she had been given over the years. They were key characters in this particular game.

One day I came in to get the list for groceries and noticed they were all gone - at least the ones that had been in the living room. I asked where they were and she smiled and said, "The children have been naughty. Come and see where they are."

I walked into the bedroom and she had arranged them all over the room. One bear sat with his face in the corner. Several animals sat upon the bed in a circle with a doll facing them. Several more from her collection were on the floor, with one particular panda bear upside down. I had to ask "What are they doing?" That was just what she had hoped I would do.

"Well, the bear in the corner was sassy. The others did not do their lessons and so the dolly on the bed is reading to them because she is the teacher. The panda is standing on his head showing off."

I knew she had not lost her mind.

She thought of a way to play, a way to have fun. It was adorable, and honestly, I could not wait for the next time to see what she had prepared for me. Why not play? Each time she would have everyone in a different place, a different pose, and with a different story.

Each story got progressively a little longer and also a little better. It was lovely to see her have so much fun. WHY NOT?

No matter how old a person gets there is always a bit of a child inside. Sometimes you just need to awaken the child inside your mama, and the one inside you, as well. Mama woke up her own child! Fun lightens many burdens.

When my daughter came to see Mama one of her visits, Mama included her in this particular game. At first Fawn thought her Ganny had lost her mind. She looked at me with eyes the size of tennis balls. Quickly she realized it was a game and got right into the spirit of it.

Games are fun, and whatever you choose, it will break the monotony of a senior's day. The stuffed animal game inspired imagination. We also played Scrabble. That particular game kept her mind sharp and was a reminder to keep her vocabulary and spelling sharp. She was too funny! We caught her cheating one time but Fawn and I just smiled and later agreed - so what! We were there to have fun.

When I was a child, she taught me Charleston in the living room and we danced and danced. Though she was unable to do what she had always done, once in a while I would put my arms around her and we would just stand and move to the rhythm of the song. She loved doing that. It was fun for me too.

Crossword puzzles, puzzles in general, monopoly, whatever game you choose just remember: during that time her thoughts will be on the game, and not on the pains of aging. A busy mind has no time for thoughts of loneliness, or boredom. Fun times like these will lighten the burden for you, as well.

Chapter 7

Chapter 7

Ascension

Death comes to us all. It is just a matter of time. Many seniors do not want to discuss death at all. Whether it is fear that keeps them from discussing it openly or simply a personal choice, at some point it must be discussed.

Mama said, "We have to talk about dying. It is the natural progression of things and I'm not afraid of dying. It is the living that is tough!" She was right.

Death is around us all the time. We see it in the movies, read about it in the newspapers, and once in a while are witness to it, simply by accident.

Death will come to us all. No one knows the expiration date on each individual life. This year I have lost both my siblings.

My older sister lost her life to cancer. Her husband joined her ten days later. Five months after her deah, just a few days ago, my beloved twin brother left for his spirit to return to God, from whence it came.

Death is not easy, as I have said,

nonetheless, it is something expected at some point. We all face death sooner or later.

There is no need for you to be unprepared with your mama or daddy – or any older person we have in the circle of our lives. We know it is probably sometime on the horizon, sooner than later.

People who are in the profession of elder caregivers see death on a regular basis with clients. One of the hard facts regarding the timing of death, is that when it really happens close to us, NONE OF US expects the day of reckoning to be upon us as "quickly" as it seems to happen. Death is always a shock.

When it comes to a dying parent, the scenario can be extremely difficult. I knew Mama would die one day. She wanted to talk about it.

It eased her mind to be able to share her thoughts and wishes. I swear I thought Mama would live to be at least ninety.

Even with her severe osteoporosis and osteoarthritis and her other physical disabilities, her blood pressure was great, her blood work excellent, her cholesterol low, and even the doctor felt she was doing extraordinarily well for an eighty-three-year-old woman.

Within the week she was gone.

I had suggested Mama see her physician early in the week. I thought perhaps she was coming down with a cold or something. She seemed listless and seemed only to want to sleep. I was afraid she was becoming dehydrated and was not eating enough as well.

I contacted her doctor. He agreed a checkup might be in order. This time she did not fight me on seeing the doctor.

After his examination her doctor suggested she stay overnight in the hospital.

Ordinarily she fought even going to visit someone at the hospital, but she trusted my judgment and liked and trusted the physician. She wanted to feel better.

Prior to admittance she twisted her back and injured herself again. I believe it was a fracture of one or two ribs. She was in terrible pain and said she would have the doctor check it out.

Once she was admitted to the hospital, we found out she was dehydrated and had a urinary tract infection. After the second day of treatment the nurse called me and said "Your mother is not acting very nice. Actually she is very naughty. She pulled her catheter out and she says she is ready to go home." OUCH!

I immediately went to the hospital and there

she lay very weak, yet anxious to go home. I honestly felt she was not ready, so I agreed to take her home only if the doctor said she was well enough the next morning on his rounds.

That evening she seemed to be drifting in and out of another world and seemed to be hallucinating. I thought perhaps they had increased the Dilaudid, a derivative of Morphine.

Though her pain had diminished I was concerned. She just did not look well.

Bright and early the next morning Mama called and said the doctor had released her. I was shocked.

Dr. Campbell was very thorough though and so I trusted she was okay. I kept to our agreement. I think she was able to "put on the dog" for him and make him think she was well enough to get out of there.

To me she looked weak and her color was pale, but she was ready to go home. I was upset as I gathered her things and began to wheel her to the car. She knew it without me saying a word. I was very worried.

She was just worried about getting home. She told me in a very sober tone, "Hospitals kill people. I do not want to die in a hospital."

When we settled her into her recliner, I put a movie in the DVD and told her I would go to get a few groceries and be right back with a bit of supper too. She smiled and told me to go.

I just guessed she was tired and weak. I returned about thirty minutes later and she was still sitting in the chair with the VCR control in her hand. She said she could not remember how to turn the movie on and so she just sat and waited for me.

I could understand. I never can really say I know how to use the remote on ANY of our electronic gadgets.

I attributed the confusion to the medications, though I thought it was unusual for her to be so out of it - no matter what the medication.

Mama slept fairly well overnight. I insisted on staying with her as I knew she wanted to go to the hairdresser the next day. After coffee and a bite to eat, I told her I was not going to take her as I felt she was not strong enough. She insisted. She looked at me with those pale blue eyes and I felt the fire begin to burn, so I agreed to take her.

When we arrived at the beauty shop, she usually used her walker to enter and leave. She did not want the girls to see the wheelchair.

I drew the line there and took out the wheelchair. She finally said she would let me use it though she hated me at the moment.

I do understand now having had to use both a walker and a wheelchair. It is a humbling experience, and of course if you can get away with not needing the help of those tools, it is better for the self-esteem; or perhaps it is vanity.

As we age it is natural to try to stay as healthy and vibrant as possible.

Nonetheless, when we begin to need to use tools to help us, it does become more of a task accepting of the challenges.

I did kind of let loose on Mama one afternoon. When I found out that she had politely told the nurse that had called that she did not need daily visits to check up on her. The doctor had arranged for this and I thought it a good idea. She flatly said the nurse was not needed. I let go!

I sat down on the floor near her chair and began to cry. I put my head on her lap and wailed, "I am so tired. I wish I could just be your daughter again."

She smoothed down my hair and said, "I am so sorry honey. I don't want any trouble. I would not intentionally do anything to make you upset."

I could have cut my own tongue out!

The minute I heard my very own words, it was too late. I told her I was so sorry and that I was just worried about her and exhausted.

She did immediately forgive me, of course. I felt terrible for putting her in a position of feeling badly for needing to ask for my help. I actually really felt awful. I still do!

Growing old has so many potential causes for battles. It is important to pick the ones that are most important to fight. I went home for the night still feeling terrible about letting loose on Mama.

Saturday morning came and I got up early to go to Mama's, as I had promised I would do the night before.

She still insisted on living alone at eighty-three, and was still one of the strongest willed persons I had ever known. For me if often meant three or four trips a day from my house to hers, but I tried to tie the visits into my own plans.

We had a wonderful day this particular day, though she was very tired and not up to par. Her pain level seemed quite under control and she was much more lucid. We read the Bible and talked about many spiritual things. When I was a child Mama often paraphrased things from the Bible but

I did not know, at the time, the wisdom was all biblically based.

She had lost her battle with osteoporosis. By the time we were told what it was it was, it was far too late to do anything about it. From her appearance that day I felt she had fractured more ribs on both sides now. I noticed she had lost another inch or so in height just overnight.

She did not complain about the pain. She walked slowly with the walker that also made into a seat. After having it for a couple of years she turned to me and said, "I am sorry I fought using this for so long honey. It is wonderful and I have really needed it!"

She asked me why I had stuck with her so long and I laughed and told her that I actually remembered being an infant.

You waited until you thought I was sleeping and then picked me up and cuddled me while whispering in my ear - "I love you. You will never leave me." I assured her it had worked perfectly and I would never leave her. She smiled.

She walked to the kitchen and hovered over the walker and sink. As she clutched the counter, she bent over and laid her head and arm on it. She was so tired. I could see the entire outline of her spine. It seemed so much worse than the day before.

I placed my hand gently on her back, rubbing up and down her little frame.

"Will I ever get well?" she asked. I promised her she would. I crossed my fingers behind my back. I did not believe she could get well.

We sat at the kitchen table as we had done many times before. She talked about seeing daddy again. She asked what would happen if she went crazy and possibly shrank down to a very, very tiny person.

I told her I would still have big love for her and if she got too small, I would put her in my pocket and carry her around with me. She smiled.

"Oh baby," she said, "I do not know what I did to deserve your love." I sure did. She shared her unconditional love, her laughter, and her time. She was generous and would find money if someone needed it, even if it left her finances depleted.

One time Mama even brought home a young woman who had recently arrived to the USA from Germany. Mama was at the bus station to meet a family member when a bewildered young woman stepped off the bus. She could speak little English. Mama asked her where she would live.

She said she did not know. She lived with us for months while Mama helped her with English, a resume, and ideas on where she would live.

The young woman insisted an exchange was fair, and she did some ironing and sewing for Mama. Mama told her it was not necessary, but she wanted to give back in some way.

Ultimately Mama made sure she was in a safe small apartment and was ready to apply for work. She even made sure she had food in the cupboards and money in her pocket.

That was just the tip of the iceberg in mentioning the wonderful things that made Mama loved by all! It was her heart and her love that won our hearts.

That day Mama thought she was losing her mind. Her pain was light but she told me there were people all over the house who were trying to make her think they were real. She said she knew they were not but still it concerned her.

She told me someone was waving at her. I told her to wave back as it was probably her angel. She smiled and waved to other characters that were in her vision only on that day.

Late in the afternoon she said there were ropes, string, and thread all over the house, and they were all tying together to make one cord.

She asked me if she was going mad. I told her no because if she were she would not be aware she was hallucinating.

I suggested perhaps the effect of her morphine was more intense because of a higher dosage given to her while in the hospital. She was so exhausted.

I told her I would spend the night and she said, 'NO! GO HOME! I am fine. Your husband is coming in tonight.

If you promise you will come over in the morning to balance the check book, it will be perfect. I cannot seem to balance it at all anymore." She chuckled.

Reluctantly I agreed but told her I would tuck her in bed first. I helped her with her favorite pajamas and she lay down in her bed. She looked so tiny. I brushed the hair from her face and leaned down and our lips kissed ever so gently.

I was grateful Mama still had her wits about her. Her little body was diminishing but her mind and intellect were still very sharp most of the time.

She often wondered if she would trade her mind for a strong body. I told her I wished she did not have either, but was so grateful we could still verbally play and laugh. I was glad we could still communicate.

As I opened the front door, I paused, and said, "I love you Mama. See you in the morning." I heard her say, "I love you too baby. Goodbye for now."

That was the last goodbye. She died some time very early that next morning.

YOU NEVER KNOW how long you will get to share time with your mama. Death comes to each of us. It is the end of our presence on this earth.

I am grateful to know within my heart and Spirit though, that this it is not the end. I am so confident I would bet the remainder of my life on that fact.

We take for granted the fact we seem to have unlimited time and then in a moment time is no longer. For the time you have remaining on this planet please remember, once your Mama is gone she will never be with you again in this way.

You will with sorrow, remember every time with her you could have done better. You will recall every good deed, but always feel you could have done more.

I wish I had done so much more.

" Then shall the dust return to the earth as it was; and the spirit shall return unto God who gave it."

     Ecclesiastes 12:7

"… man lieth down and rises not: till the heavens be no more, they shall not awake, nor be raised out of their sleep."

     Job 14:12

"Now faith is the substance of things hoped for, the evidence of things not seen."

     Hebrews 11:1

Chapter 8

Chapter 8
Bottom of the Barrel, the Top of the Line

Dying is not the end of the story. It does not even come close to a quick exit. The last part of the process will come to you over the next months. Many things come to fruition and there will be transitions for all members of the family that are close to your mama. witness a death, the vision can be staggering to you consciously and unconsciously.

Death for the living is never easy. Whether your loved one dies in a hospital or in your arms, if you have never been present to

I was not with Mama when she died. I had done what she wanted me to do, however in all honesty I wanted to go home for the night too. I never once thought of her dying.

Many nights I had spent the night on Mama's fold out couch and it was awfully uncomfortable. Every time I heard movement or a noise I was up and awake and ready to do what I could to help. I needed to sleep in my own bed.

Mama had told me to call before I came over so she could put on the coffee and fix up a bit.

Michael had come in late and so I sneaked out of the bedroom and called from the kitchen. No answer. I rang several times with intervals in between the calls. It never occurred to me that she was gone.

As I was writing a note to let Michael know I was leaving, I heard from the bedroom a groggy, "Go on sweetheart. Call me if you need me and I will come on over."

He had always been there with me for mama. I heard a loud snore from both Michael and the dog! "Good", I thought, "He needs the rest."

It was not unusual for mama to be slow to pick up the phone, so I was not really worried.

The sky was dotted with a few clouds and the crisp feel of fall was better than a cup of coffee. As I was on my way, I asked God to help Mama deal with the great pain she had been dealing with for years now. She was a brave little soldier.

I knocked on the door. No answer. I knocked again. She did not answer. I found Mama's key and quietly opened the door. The curtains were still closed and the silence bellowed throughout the apartment.

As I walked through the living room, to her bedroom, there was a strange emptiness in the apartment. The quiet was deafening.

"Mama, where are you?" I yelled. No answer. Mama's Spirit was gone. I could feel the absence of it.

I looked in her room and there she lay on the floor next to her bed. My heart pounded as if it would burst from my chest as I yelled and tried to revive her, but I knew she was gone.

Her body lay on the floor almost like a little pad of melted butter. It was Mama's body, but it was not Mama. I knew for sure.

There was a spot of blood on her forehead. It was as if she sat up in bed, and her little body just dropped to the ground, with her head grazing the night table.

I do not really know how long I was there. I tried to lift her to the bed, but her body

was like a rag doll, and it was impossible for me to do. I cried and cried and then I got a warm washcloth to gently wash her face.

I had seen her get a warm washcloth and wash her face, first thing in the morning, so many times in her life She said it woke her up and made her open her eyes! I washed the blood off gently. I think I was wishing she would open her eyes.

I brushed her hair off of her face, as I had done the evening before, and slowly got up.

I did not want to leave Mama. I did not want her to leave me. The apartment already was void of her Spirit. It was so silent. I thought about our conversations the previous night- the ropes and the angels.

Now it all made sense.

I walked out of the apartment and leaned on the apartment building. Looking at the morning clouds scatter and dissipate, I thought "It's over. Mama's gone."
I felt numb all over. It was such a strange sensation. Within few minutes I called my husband. All I had to do was say, "I need you." He said he would be there in minutes. He was but those minutes in between seemed like a lifetime.

The breeze I took a deep breath as I thought it is over. No more pain for Mama. No more Mama in my lifetime.

I sighed blew my tears across my cheeks. a sigh of relief that she would feel no more pain, a sigh of sorrow realizing she was really gone, and that same moment I heard the motorcycle come around the corner.

As I stood at the door waiting for him, a lifetime of memories washed over me. I wept and I was in disbelief, all at the same time. Michael came to me and I fell into his arms weeping. He already knew.

Michael had never faced a situation with the loss of a loved one.

He had never lost anyone, nor seen anyone dead. I had lost my father some years ago, but I was in another state providing for my family, so I was unable to come to mama.

He came through for me, as he always does. I could not stand the thought of Mama being on the floor the way she was. I asked him to please pick her up and put her on the bed. I do not know how he managed to do it, but he did. He lifted her as if she was a feather, and he laid her gently down on the bed. At that moment she seemed to exhale right into his face. It startled him but he never mentioned it until later. We were told it was the oxygen being released that had been trapped in her little body.

He proceeded, without one word from me, to make her comfortable. He drew her blanket u placed her arms gently by her sides, leaving her sweet little face exposed. Thank God her eyes were already closed when I discovered her. I just froze in place when he moved her. I watched my darling husband carry my beloved mama to her bed and gently help her for the last time.

Michael grabbed my hand and we went to sit at the kitchen table, now realizing we needed to notify the family. Before that, we called 911. The operator told us the paramedics would be there shortly and also the fire department would come.

I found it is a standard procedure when a body is reported. They were quite professional but actually also profoundly sensitive to our loss. They could see how upset we were and after checking Mama they said we needed to call the coroner.

He arrived within the hour and to my amazement, the coroner told us he could have arrested Michael right there for moving the body I was shocked but he said in these cases you could be handling a murder. That is an appalling fact. He said some elderly people have been murdered by an abusive friend or relative simply because they were "too much trouble."

I emphatically let him know how I could not stand seeing my Mama laying on the floor that way. He mellowed a bit and aid if we contacted Mama's physician and he would agree to sign the death warrant there would be no problems.

We spoke to Mama's physician, and he said absolutely he would sign, but he was even surprised at Mama's death. "She seemed so good at the hospital when I signed her release." he said. I knew he was right. She had fooled us both! I believe she knew she was close to death and she wanted to go home.

The coroner recommended a local mortuary. Though he was not supposed to do so he said they were very family oriented, and really wonderful people. Within minutes after calling them

Mama's body was gone. Now we faced the monumental task of informing the family.

No matter how prepared you think you are, when death knocks at the door of your parent, your life changes forever.

Temporarily you have hit the bottom of the barrel if you have had a close relationship with them. Even if it were not as close as mine, you will still find yourself in the midst of new territory.

I stress temporarily because as humans we have the power to recover from almost anything. There are steps to mourning and it will take time.

Healing does not mean forgetting. It means being able to move on and begin again to celebrate life at some point.

The point this happens is different timing for all of us.

I realize I speak from a position of one who dearly loved and respected her parents. The reason I write from the point of view of caring for your mother, is because that I cared for my mother for ten years.

For clarification I know there are things we have not touched upon, but this book is written from personal experiences and lessons, and therein, I cannot presume to embellish on that which I have not experienced.

It is all unfamiliar territory, but God does give us insight in we pray and listen.

This book is intended to make your life easier and the life of your mother more fulfilled her last years. Many of the tips and techniques reviewed in this book are applicable to both male and female.

Each scenario changes according to personalities and experiences, but there are some things that are common to all human beings.

Love is your number one strength. Love never fails. God never fails. No doubt though, when a loved one dies it is life altering.

One by one we contacted members of the immediate family.

We sat in Mama's kitchen making phone calls and we looked at one another still numb in disbelief.

We knew it was coming, but when the time actually came, it was still unexpected. In reflection of that time, I believe we both were in shock.

One of the very first things I learned after mama's death was that in dealing with other family members you must become strong and positive. It will not only ease the pain for them, but it may help guide you to focus and is actually a way to begin the healing.

Suddenly you are the matriarch for this time period.
You are not in charge of you family members for the balance of their lives, but at this particular passing, you are either in charge of what happens as a positive force, or you

are a sorrowful and pitiful little soul.
I am not saying you cannot cry with your siblings and family.   Nor am I saying you will not have rough days. However, in order to help so many individuals, try to accept this passage with strength and grace.

You will need to be a good leader.

We contacted all close members of the family that night to let them know Mama was gone. Each person was caught off guard. No one really expected Mama's death. She never let most family members know how bad she was feeling. The truth is no one really ever expects death at the moment it happens.

We have a tendency to assume that life goes on and on, and death really only happens to others.

After notifying the family my darling husband and I went from room to room in Mama's apartment, gathering special things that she had designated for each person. I do not think it was necessary to do it so quickly but in a way, it helped us to reconcile her death as we walked and talked. this was what she had wanted.

We opened her lock box. She had designated me as the person who would take charge of everything and do what she asked. To our amazement she had saved a thousand dollars. It sat on top, in one-hundred-dollar bills.

A note was attached to it that explained the money was for the cremation and any expense that occurred.

We were stunned. On her limited income, she must have been saving for a couple of years. Even in death Mama was thoughtful and caring for us.

I couldn't believe she had done this, and truthfully it would have been tough for us to carry it at the time.

The cremation wound up costing the entire one thousand dollars. Today the price has gone to a minimum of fifteen hundred for simply the cremation. It is much more expensive for a casket and funeral services.

Family members will respond differently. You will find un-expected guests flying in to offer sympathy and attend any service to be held. Others that you assume might attend could surprise you and not be at the gathering at all.

You must have great understanding about this as we all have the right to respond individually, the right to live our lives, and choose how we behave in such a situation.

Family members may not be in a financial position to come, or work may keep someone from coming. You never know the circumstances of another's life.

Whatever the family decides to do individually does not lessen the love they felt for the deceased. Be respectful and supportive of each person's decision. Some people simply cannot imagine seeing someone they loved lying in a coffin.

Some people might not be able to afford a trip or even flowers. During this time of loss be generous with your breadth of understanding and give unconditional love. This time is no time for judgments or bickering.

It is a time for love, mourning your loss, and for the healing to begin. The coroner had been right in recommending this particular mortuary.

"We see so many families going through unnecessary expense in these situations." Mr. Dahl said.

"May I suggest you bypass the embalming of your mother's body? We feel it wrong to fill the body full of chemicals. We are able to keep your mother's body very nice for the family gathering, if you choose to have one. We will make her look lovely, and it will save a great expense.

You will have a viewing room where you will all gather to honor her for the last time." We thought his suggestions were fine and very kind. We agreed.

Whether you must arrange for a funeral,

purchase a casket, have a memorial service, or cremate your parent, remember, the time you spend with her while she is alive is the most important time of all. Love her before she is gone.

The family arrived. It was very difficult to greet family with tears instead of the usual happy greetings, and initially we were all tearful and at a loss for exactly what to say. Expect those moments when you feel you have lost control, but endeavor to help one another be strong. Hugs will help. Even for those who normally are not huggers, the hugs and compassion you share will help to heal everyone.

Just when the tone was so terribly sad someone would bring up something mama did or said that was just too funny to stay sad. She told us all in order to live happy you must develop a sense of humor. You can turn things around to recall the joys that were shared by all.

I was very fortunate as the think I came from the womb smiling. Then I was reared in a home where sense of humor and love were king and queen.

God gave me a positive attitude too, and through the years, though I faced many horrific times in my life, as many of us do, I worked hard to keep positive.

I also believe God and prayer have been major factors in my healing from injuries and of my handling of traumatic situations throughout my life.

It was wonderful too that my Mama and Daddy worked hard to stay positive. They both had wonderful sense of humors. Our family spent many hours playing and laughing together. Those times were blessings to remember.

With technology accelerating at such a pace, try to remember to have family time free from technology; perhaps a technology free room in your home.

Initially there will be a brief consolation blitz. When people arrive at your home be grateful for those who came, and if need be, put them to work!

There will be flowers, food, hotel rooms to book, and room to make in your own home.

You have not only lost your parent but for a while, you will become group coordinator, hostess, chef, and housing director. It may also be your position to arrange for the burial or cremation, any services that will be held, and the reading of the will.

I thank God every day of my life that my beloved husband of over thirty-five years was there to help me every step of the way. He was willing to do whatever I needed, and capable of handling of many of the details I had forgotten.

He is a blessing to me, and was surely one for my Mama. He loved her dearly.

At the end of each day no matter how trying the days were, I could count on falling into his arms taking comfort in his love and strong nature. He was will to do whatever I needed and capable of taking care of many details I had forgotten.

Loosing Mama was ONE of the greatest losses I have suffered in this lifetime. I worked hard to remember I was not the only one to suffer a great loss. Many people have lost children and entire families.

Mama told me, "I am old, and in terrible pain. I am ready any time. It is the natural way of things." Though we all will get old and die, in this case, Mama's statements did let me know she was ready, which helped me keep a perspective of the facts blending intellect with emotions, and tempering my grief.

I still am not ready for the loss of my twin brother, which happened a few days ago. I feel like I am caught between this planet and another. I am in between the red zone and the yellow zone. Somehow, even with the loss of my father and mother, the loss of my sister, and especially my twin, have left me not yet on solid terrafirma. Perhaps because the loss of my siblings has been so close in time. Both passed in a period of the last five months. I will continue and trust that "diversion" is a great way to begin to handle thoughts one ordinarily cannot manage quickly.

Flowers and food came in from Mama's neighbors and friends. The telephone rang constantly with support from those who were unable to attend Mama's last rites.

I speak only of taking care of Mama, as I have reiterated, it does not mean daddy was not wonderful, or that I would not have taken care of him, if needed. But daddy was killed over thirty years ago.

It was sudden, not a lingering and painful degeneration of the body as Mama was forced to endure. Daddy did not have to suffer the process of aging, but his death was totally unnecessary.

An inept surgeon killed him and though Mama pursued a lawsuit so the physician would not kill anyone else, it could not bring daddy back.

She won the lawsuit, but the surgeon moved to Canada and began operating once again - even though he had several wrongful death lawsuits pending here in the states.

What transpired during the next hours and days was surely a credit to the love Mama taught us all.

When all the family members who were coming had arrived, we sat in a circle in our living room. None of us had really planned that first evening. The only thing I knew for sure was that at some point I would play the tape Mama had left for us. I was then going to give each person a specific item Mama had designated for him or her.

What they did not know was that I had put several items with the ones Mama had designated, so that each family member had a remembrance from Mama. She would have been pleased.

No one felt unloved. Mama really loved us all and I knew she would want that. Each gift was s was truly appreciated.

That evening we chatted and spontaneously laughed thinking of many of the humorous and wonderful times we had shared with Mama. We cried and consoled one another at her passing.

At one point in the evening my twin brother said his daughter would like to sing a song to honor her grandmother. She sang "Amazing Grace" and it was the perfect choice! I do not believe one person was without tears during those moments.

After the sweet vocal tribute to Mama, I explained in detail the day before Mama's passing.

I chose not to reveal that I had found Mama on the floor. I felt this time was not the place to for anyone to hear those details - maybe never. My husband concurred.

It was a year or two afterward I did tell my siblings. They were grateful I had not shared that during the family gathering.

We had made a wise decision. The shock of her death was plenty to handle for everyone. The vision of her dying peacefully in her bed was more settling to the family.

Her wish was that no one would see her after death, but her generosity of her Spirit came to light again when she let me know, if anyone chose to see her body after she died, it would be okay.

In keeping that lovely sense of humor of hers, she also told me one time, "I understand if I have not seen someone for a while, they might want to see me one more time, and since I don't have to look, I guess it is okay!" She giggled. I did too.

God gave me so much help in caring for Mama. Often ideas popped into my head I never contemplated on my own. One idea was for Mama to make a cassette tape for the family to hear her voice saying goodbye to all. She balked at first, but spent quite a bit of time, over weeks, making a tape for the family to hear.

It was touching to see the faces on of family as they heard Mama's sweet voice one more time.

He called her phone and when the answering machine picked up the call, he simply left a message saying, "I just wanted to hear your voice one more time Ganny. I love you."

When I heard the phone message he had left to her, it made me cry. I still cry upon reflection of the love he felt for her.

Ganny was a name Mama's first grandchild called her and it just stuck to her over the years.

She had always given special attention to each member of the family. She shared unconditional love and whatever else was needed, whether it was material things, the building up of true self-esteem, or a good lecture.

She even made the boys go into her small yard once and pick a switch out of the tree.

The switch was just for a swat, a firm reminder to adhere to the rules. A small amount of pain with no injury, love, and wise words can teach wisdom to children.
They loved her so much. They respected her and learned from her.

Unless there is to be a large gathering of family for meals and restaurants have been booked, everyone will just expect food to be provided by you. I don't know if expect is the right word - most people are grieving and given that, they may not even think of food cost and preparation.

I believe the problem with many teens today is they have no respect for anything, nor or fear of reprisal when they are out of line. I do not mean beatings. I mean firm reminders that actions bring consequences. I am not alone in thinking this way.

The Bible reiterates if we do not discipline young children, they will not learn to take responsibility for their actions.

That doesn't mean everyone should not share in the cost and help with the tasks before and after the meals. You can make it peaceful and visit all the while.

Most people are amiable sharing the cost, and you'll find many friends and family will bring casseroles and other food to help provide for all.

Each situation is different however, and it may be necessary for you to guide family members to become part of the task force.

Working together can bring a feeling of family unity. This will help create a flow that can allow any past problems between people to be forgotten, or at least placed on hold until another time.

Our gathering was small and we did enjoy a bit of alcohol, and perhaps, a bit too much! Emotional times are not the time to overindulge. Truly there is never a good time to overindulge in alcohol. We were lucky as we just laughed and didn't have any problems.

Keep in mind, alcohol may seem to take the edge off, but if truth be told, people often don't know when to stop. When the effects of alcohol wears off, emotions drop, and depression usually follows.

The day of the viewing my husband and my precious daughter, Fawn, came with me to make sure everything was ready. We had been the three people who had spent the majority of time with Mama the last years of her life. I felt we should have some moments alone with her together.

Michael had been with Mama for all her surgeries the last years, right beside me. Even if he was driving cross-country at the time, when I needed him or Mama did, he would break his back getting home to us.

Our daughter had shared many hours with her Ganny. When she lived at home it was easier, but when she went to study at college, she made extra efforts to spend time with her. They played cards, talked about love and life, and they even had a few hot disagreements! But their time was invaluable to both of them.

It was so important to Mama that Fawn, being a young adult. took the time and made the effort to spend quality time with her Ganny. We held each other's hands as we entered the room Mr. Dahl called the "quiet room".

We were on a mission to say our goodbyes first, and then to finish preparing Mama for the family viewing, which was to be held later that afternoon.

I selected a pretty blouse that Mama had worn so many times. She thought it was lovely when she first purchased it, and so did I.

It had bright colors and a few sequins. She had not been specific about things for the viewing, but I felt certain she would have been pleased. She was so still. This was the first time in my life I had seen anyone dead, except of course, when I found mama initially. I think I was kind of in shock.

Mama was so still and quiet. I knew this was just the body that housed her Spirit, but still, it was Mama's earthly home.

The staff at the funeral home had placed her gently on a gurney covered with a soft sheet. They dressed her and really did most of the preparation. She looked as if she was sleeping. "Just one thing missing," I thought. It was her eyebrows.

All my life I had known Mama to be almost traumatized had she been preparing to go someplace and she was not able to use her eyebrow pencil to fill in her brows. She was not a vain person at all.

She felt it was her duty to look as pleasant as possible, to make us proud of her as our mama.

She had been a professional executive secretary to some very important people in the Garden Grove Union High School District.

When she was sixteen, she had tweezed her eyebrows almost off. It was the fashion of the day. The brows were but a memory. She would ask me when she finished filling in her eyebrows with makeup, "Are my eyebrows okay?"

"Yes mama," I replied. She looked so cute and I loved her to pieces.

Over the years I remember her purchasing pencils of different colors. It was probably the most important primping she did. I took an auburn eyebrow pencil, and a brown one, and made sure the remainder of the family saw her with her "eyebrows on". I think she would have been pleased.

It was a total surprise to me when our daughter leaned down and kissed her Ganny right on the lips. I thought she would be shy about touching her, because this was the first event in her young life, she had actually seen anyone dead in person.

It was particularly difficult for her as Ganny was someone whom she treasured deeply.

I mentioned how surprised I was and Fawn just replied, "She was my grandma – my Ganny. I loved her with all my heart, and this is the little body she lived in all the time I have been alive. I am not afraid of it now, though I know her Spirit is not here."

I was so proud of her mature thinking during the most stressful incident thus far in her young life.

I thought of the holidays when Fawn suggested she and I dressed up and she knocked at Ganny's door. She was so surprised we then sang Christmas carols. We were not a choir, that is for sure, but Mama's excitement and joy was beyond the happiness we had hoped she would feel.

Fawn did have a lovely voice. Still does. I never tire of her sing. She was always was So kind and did lovely things for her grandma too.

Both my sons were unable to attend, but they adored Ganny and I knew their hearts were deeply at a loss with her passing. My eldest son was unable to come as he was working hard to support his wife and three children, and he lived on the east coast.

The cost of the flights for him alone was very high and he did not want to leave his young family. I understood. He just asked me to send something that she loved. I sent her pajamas and a few other items.

I

It was probably a year or two after mama passed that my daughter could finally bring herself to wash a sweatshirt that had been mama's sweatshirt.

She always held it close to her and she said, "It smells like Ganny." Then she would hold it even closer to her and smile. I still use Ponds dry skin cream to this day as it smells just like mama.

The remainder of the family arrived shortly and we stood near Mama. She was the matriarch of our clan. She was the one person whom everyone could count on no matter what the circumstance.

She had given each one of us absolute unconditional love and affection. She had also given each of us time and a special relationship. She also had given us each a lecture at one time or another!

The ultimate unconditional love and hope she felt for each one of us was implicitly shown one time when a member of the family got into a bit of trouble with the law. Without thinking she signed an agreement that put her home up as a guarantee for bail. She said she knew the boy and that he would not run, and that he would be a great man someday. She was right, and today he actually owns his own business, and is a deeply caring father and grandfather.

As Daddy would have said about Mama, "What a gal."

No one directed us that day. We instinctively stood around in a circle leaving space for Mama to be in the center of the circle. We joined hands. She always made room for us in her life, and now we were together to honor her, and to say goodbye for now.

One by one each of us began to say something special about Mama. Each person shared some of the things that made her so important to us. My husband is a very private person, but it was his turn share his sentiment and of what mama had meant to him.

"Marjorie could be a real handful too. She was full of something wild and wonderful. She gave each of us some trouble at times, but we loved her for, and in spite of it. She was usually right on the money.

"Marjorie could be a real handful too. She was full of something wild and wonderful.

She gave each of us some trouble at times, but we loved her for, and in spite of it. She was usually right on the money. I really will miss her." We all smiled and nodded.

At one point my sister said she wanted to sing a special song that she had meant to share with Mama. Mama always encouraged us, each one in his or her special talent or love. Lesley had a lovely voice but this day, as she sang, her voice trembled so much we could barely understand what the words were. She finished and cried. We all cried.

Several family members sang. We said prayers individually.

The Lord's Prayer we all said together.

It was a marvelous ode to our love for God and Mama. Everyone in the clan believes in God, but our modes of transportation to reach Him unique in many family members.

We were Christians, followers of Parmahansa Yogananda, Jehovah's Witness', and other groupings of God's peoples. That day no one touted declarations saying, "I am the right one in my beliefs", nor questioned another's offering. It was a melding of love empowered by God.

It was a time to love one another, and let judgments flee.

The celebration of Mama's life and our last time together with her came to an end as simply as it began that day. As we left , we bid her goodbye and hugged to share the joy, and sadness of the moment.

We returned home and the wake began. Mama had told us she wanted a celebration of her life when she died.

If you opt to have alcohol available make sure no one drinks and drives. I am not saying this is a great time to party-hearty, but inevitably some groups do just that. The death of a loved one is listed high up on the biggest stresses of a person's life.

We all handle tragedy differently, but the last thing anyone on the planet would want is a ticket for drunk driving – or worse, to hurt someone else by causing an accident. You and your mate or partner are really in charge of making sure this does not happen.

That evening we drank a glass of champagne to toast Mama.

During the course of the evening, we provided lots of food, some wine, coffee, tea, carbonated drinks and of course the true nectar of God, water. We bonded again and it was a lovely reunion at a difficult time.

Many of our guests had planes to catch, or had to leave for other obligations.

My twin brother and his wife, my sister and her husband, and my husband and myself were left to divide the remainder of Mama's possessions.

The next day we began the task of breaking down the things in Mama's apartment. Mama's love trickled down permeating the surroundings. What could have been a grab-fest nightmare for some relatives was a calm and mellow day.

The division of assets reflected the love we all felt for Mama, and there were no squabbles about "who wanted what."

There was no training manual for this job. My sister-in-law would say, "Why don't you keep this?" (No particular item; just an example).

If I wanted it, I would thank her and ask if she was sure she didn't want it. My brother would look at something my sister might be looking at, and he would say she should have it. And so it went.

For several days the conversation was just that. No one grabbed. No one was hurt or felt left out of the disbursement.

Try to remember that your mama's possessions are NOT your mama. Owning a material possession that was Mama's never brings her back to you.

The only thing bickering over material possessions will do is reflect a lack of respect for her life and the love you felt for her.

We all chatted and one or two of us would walk to a room and we simply remembered earlier times, times of laughter and times we shared individually with Mama. It was lovely.

At one point I looked at the drapery in Mama's room and it brought tears to my eyes. There was still a shoelace tied to the drapery so that mama could reach the cords to close it. She had lost so much height due to her crumbling frame she was unable to open and close the drapes had she not thought of a way to manage it.

My sister held me tightly. I cried.

And so it was the majority of the day. We reveled in the warmth and personality Mama had created in her small apartment. She had made a home for all the family to visit and enjoy. We thought of the good years we were able to share.

We laughed and cried. If someone admired something, another person would suggest, "You keep it. You really seem to like it. Mama would have wanted that."

Late in the afternoon my siblings and husband and I sat at the kitchen table and I read the handwritten will.

Late in the afternoon my siblings and husband and I sat at the kitchen table and I read the handwritten will. Many items were not mentioned, but there was no question about Mama's wishes. We always had been brought up with love and trust in each other.

The kind sharing of her worldly material possessions will in the long run, leave you with more within your Spirit that they can provide in any material value. Regardless of the value of items, the increase in peace and growth of your character will pay off for your entire lifetime.

I can say this WITHOUT the experience of knowing how everyone would act if Mama had been rich and lived in a mansion.

I would hope and pray the courteous and generous behavior would have been similar. I know Mama would rather have thrown every single thing she owned in the trash than have a single cross word regarding who would own something.

My twin's wife at the time, was really in need of a car, as hers had just quit running. I had spoken to Mama in length about her car and she said she absolutely wanted Michael and me to sell it and use the money for the time Michael took off work when she passed, and the money we spent while entertaining our guests. I felt terrible about it though. It was something I should have just given to them no matter what! I hope God forgives me for all my selfish deeds. We could have made it without the car. Now I still think, years later, I was selfish, and should have shared.

I didn't take care of mama because I was obligated to, or because I would have felt differently if I hadn't…..I did it because I loved her and she needed my help. Simple as that!

When it comes to your parent / or parents, you do what you need to do for them because you love them! That is what WE do….

I say again, she must have known she was close to her transition. She was adamant about this. Though it was not written in the will, neither my twin nor my sister had a problem with this.

The first night after cleaning some of the apartment I went to the kitchen to get my husband to tell him it was time to quit. He was washing a few dishes. He said to me, "Your mama wouldn't have been able to sleep a wink with dirty dishes in the sink. I was just finishing them." I cried. I cried because I missed Mama and I cried because my husband had just given my Mama love and respect once again. He was correct or course!

When my sis and her hubby left on the plane for Indiana, emptiness engulfed my entire being. I was exhausted. So was my husband.

During the years I was caregiver for Mama, she and I renewed our long-time friendship, and we grew even closer in so many ways. She was my best friend, and I knew I had shared the last moments on this planet with her.

Finding her the way I did was also something I had a battle with for a long while. I could not get that picture of her on the floor out of my head out of my head.

As hard as I tried, I could not help seeing it over and over again. I think I felt terribly guilty not having been with her that night.

I felt responsible for her fall, and it took a little over two years (and lots of prayer) for the image of her to disappear. One day the image just disappeared. I tried and could not recall and it was heavenly peace.

I always remember to thank God for his graciousness and patience with me. I sighed a sigh of relief knowing that I was free of seeing Mama that way. I also let go of the guilt. Michael simply said I was not supposed to be there. I finally agreed.

I wish I had taken more time to go through Mama's paperwork and her personal effects. I believe I may and her personal effects. I believe I mhave gotten rid of some things she had written and for that, I regret

Hurrying. But we needed to have her apartment empty and clean and I was so pushed for space and time. It was something that needed to be done, so I just was not as thorough about reading all the papers she had in her files.

Take your time if you can, as you may be glad for it in future times. If you have no one to help you, focus on God. Whatever name you may call Him, He will know that you are seeking Him. Ask. He is your Father and is always close to you. Seek Him and He will find you.

Pray and turn your problems over to Him. You may not always get the answer you are seeking, but He will lead you in a direction that will be the best path for you. Practice praying and then leave your problems with God. It may take practice to have that kind of faith, but if you practice, it will become easier, and you will find the peace and help that you seek.

Even if you are unsure that you can manage things, practice thinking in positive terms. You will develop confidence along with the capabilities you so desire. You will find the more you practice thinking in positive terms, the easier it will be to empower yourself, and affect the lives of those you love.

Human beings are creatures of habit so even if you don't feel one hundred percent, speak within yourself terms that will guide you towards healing. You will create new brain cell impressions that will remind you from within that you really are healing.

When death comes it comes with many challenges to face. There are stages of grief, guilt, regrets, loneliness, and anger. At some point you will face the fact that you are now at the top of the line.

The next to die could be you or your siblings or peers. Reality roars in like a lion. This past five months the lion took a bite out of my heart. My older sister died…and so did my twin brother- just a few days ago. ☹

All go unto one place; all are of the dust, and all turn to dust again."

Ecclesiastes 3:20

"In a moment, in the twinkling of an eye, at the last trumpet, for the trumpet shall sound, and the dead shall be raised incorruptible and we shall be changed."

1 Corinthians 15:52

"I wait for the Lord, my soul doth wait, and in his word do I hope."

Psalm 130:5

Chapter 9

Chapter 9

The Last Goodbye

Mama chose to be cremated. She made it very clear to us that the way she wanted to go. She always felt cremation was less costly, less fuss, and that the ashes would take up much less space!

She said, "I think it is foolish to have a costly funeral and casket. Graveyards should be parks instead of graveyards.

Let the living have my space. People have

enough to deal with when someone dies, People have enough to deal with when someone dies. Added financial burdens should not be a part of the scenario. "

"I think it is extremely morbid to take flowers to visit a grave. My mother used to do that when daddy died and it was always the same. It brought back such sad memories of her loss. I always left my mother drowning in tears to recover all over again.

I always say to let the living enjoy the flowers and do not talk to the dead. They cannot hear us."

Mama never compromised her beliefs to placate anyone. I appreciated her thoughts on the subject and honored her request. She reminded that it says in the Bible that we "know nothing, we are sleeping, and our spirits go back to be with God until the resurrection."

No matter which choice your mama selects, no matter what your personal beliefs are, remember this last request was her decision.

Once a funeral has ended the casket will be buried, and family members will know part of all the difficult tasks are then completed.

A cremation changes does things. Afterward, within a week or so, your mama's ashes will be handed to you in the urn you selected.

There are urns that are very expensive, and those with a modest price tag. I have even heard of someone using a coffee can and asking the ashes to be placed within it.

You will need to decide the right thing to do. A friend of mine had a nephew who passed away at twenty-one years of age. He had an inoperable brain tumor. It was so sad, and when his mama received the ashes, placed the urn on the mantel with a photograph and a few small personal items next to it.

It remained there, with a small candle lit every night, for as long as I was in contact with these folks. For them it somehow helped the pain and kept his memory alive.

Some urns are put on a shelf in a closet and forgotten. It is totally the decision of the family. My friend chose to be poured out on the roots of her favorite rose tree. An elderly couple married for fifty-five years had their ashes placed near a waterfall.

When my father passed away a pilot friend of his took his ashes and threw them out of the plane over the mountains that my father loved so much.

I did a bit of research after the fact, and found the legality of disposing of the ashes might be a bit tricky. I do try to keep the laws of the land but I also believe if you have a reservation about this particular law, you need not check further than these pages, and do the will of your family member.

It is not easy to make all the decisions involving the death of your mama. Nothing in this life is easy it seems. But with prayer and love, the light on the path becomes much brighter. Keep your chin up and it will all work out fine. You simply do the best you are able, and then, as folks at the Daily Word reiterate, "Let go, and let God." Makes sense to me.

My niece and nephew thought it might be lovely to take Mama's ashes to Huntington Beach to be thrown into the ocean. She had loved the ocean, and spent most afternoons of her high school years swimming and surfing. She actually was one of the first female body surfers.

Lori and Lawrence said they felt honored to do this for Mama and me.

My nephew's flight left prior to getting the ashes back, so my sis and I carefully packed the urn and mailed the ashes priority mail. He had made arrangements to meet several family members at the end of the Huntington Beach pier, one evening.

None of these young people had ever done anything like this before. When they arrived at the pier, the fog was so thick you could not see the end of the pier. When they reached it, they clasped hands and said a prayer.

Years later we all gathered to let my sister Lesley's ashes be with mama in the surf.

It was surreal.

It had always been a family tradition to conclude any prayer with "God bless our loved ones near and far." I cannot close a prayer without saying, "In Jesus Christ's precious name I pray." I have done this since the early days of my childhood.

My nephew leaned over the pier to throw Mama's ashes into the ocean. At the very moment he did so, a seagull came up through the fog, and it flew high into the air and disappeared.

Everyone was startled but interpreted it as a beautiful message to all participating that evening. Her body was gone, but her Spirit had returned to God. It was a sign to us all.

A few months ago I lost my only sister as I

reiterated. Her husband died within a week.

They both had lung cancer, and neither of

them smoked. They died within a week of

each other.

My sis left word she wanted to have her ashes

done as had been done with mama's ashes;

thrown off of the pier in Huntington Beach.

Family all made a point of flying and driving to the destination and making sure her ashes were taken care of as she had wished. It was so amazing to see the family all together again, and we all noted, Lesley would have been thrilled. She had spoken so often of having a big family reunion. There we were, all together, loving one another and all in remembrance of her. We also committed to keep better in touch with each other.

Life passes too quickly not to make time for family. You decide to handle these last details cremation or burial, just take a breath and do the best you can. Have no regrets.

Let this be the culmination of caring for your Mama's time on this earth. Take a breath and begin again.

"Come unto me, all ye that labor, and are heavy

laden, and I will give you rest."

Matthew 11:28

"Set your affection on things above, not on

things on the earth."

Colossians 3:2

"Why are thou cast down, O my soul? And

why art thou disquieted within me? Hope in

God: for I shall yet praise Him, who is the

health of my countenance, and my God."

Psalm 43:5

"I thank my God upon every remembrance

of you…"

Philippians 1:3

Chapter 10

Chapter 10

Tragedy to Triumph

"When I die, I expect you will be a good example for your children and grandchildren. Life continues all around you, so after I go, do not go dragging around mourning forever! Get over it and begin to celebrate life again. Please baby, do this for me."

Mama always stepped out of her own pain to prime me for mine, which was to commence shortly after her own passing.

In spite of human power and wealth, all the advances in medicine, and individual creativity, we still must face aging and death. For the time being, and perhaps for all time, there is no escape from either. The hard truth is that someday your loved ones will die, and ultimately there is a place in line for you and me too.

But it will not necessarily be worse.

You have been in the process of learning your entire life. You are evolving into the person you were born to be.

When your mama dies you may wonder how you can live with the grief.

You may wonder how life will ever be the same. It will not.

The toughest of all lessons is the loss of loved ones and the recovery of others. It will be up to you whether you lose your way or rise above the stumbling blocks you now face.

There is not any fixed schedule you can mark on the calendar during the grieving process. Grief is a complicated emotion and each person's process is uniquely his or her own.

You will go through a period of shock and denial. Anger will rear its ugly head with such questions as "How dare you let this happen?" You may try to bargain with God or ask the universe to cut a deal with you.

A guaranteed emotion will be depression. Combined with exhaustion you may experience listlessness, guilt, a lack of interest in life, or you may find yourself feeling like you are ready to give up.

The last stage of grief is focusing your energy more positively, and most likely returning to setting goals in your life. You must face the loss just as you faced the job of care giving in the beginning.

You may not want this to be in this position but ultimately there are times we have no choice in the matter.

You will begin to deal with life as it is at this moment.

Truly there is no set order or time, but knowing these stages can be a helpful model to get you through your grief and sorrow. Allow yourself to grieve. The time will come when you realize the grieving period is over, and you must get on with life. Everyone's process will be different.

What influences each individual and how they are able to handle grief is a combination of his or her own personal history, religious beliefs (or not), and even cultural differences.

I was in a state of disbelief when Mama first died. As I still am about my twin, as I continue to write....

In between bouts of occasional wailing, I feel no emotion some of the time, which in turn tends to make me feel very guilty.

The same happened with mama – and again, I felt very guilty. "What is wrong with me?" I am just sort of in a zone – another realm.

When Daddy passed on, I lived out of state, and was unable to come to spend time with the family. Thankfully I had visited with him several weeks before he had passed away. When I discovered Mama was gone it really through me for a loop, as she used to say.

I might say it threw me out of the loop of living normally day by day for a while. We had been best friends and I found I could not pull myself together.

Over a period of time, I found out about the stages of grief and mourning. Time itself is a great healer.

When dealing with grief do not let other people tell you how you should act or feel. Do not let anyone put you on a time schedule, other than the one you choose for yourself. We are all different individuals. The process works differently for everyone.

Try not to pay too attention to how others think you should feel, for in doing so, you can slow the restored emotional health and peace you seek. A most important thing is become reconciled to the reality of the situation. We must grieve in order to heal. Tears and all the myriad feelings you may experience ARE NORMAL. You have not lost it!

Recovery time varies for each individual. You must be patient with yourself! Grieving is important and will help the healing.

Keep your faith strong. Stay hopeful future days will be full and happy. I believe the most powerful tool you have in healing is prayer. You will get a grip on your emotions and God does care.

When you feel like you could drop to the floor with exhaustion and emotion, instead drop to your knees and let your feelings be known to your Master.

Even if you are not very spiritual normally, give prayer a try. What is the worst that can happen?

You let out your feelings privately! Sometimes just to say a prayer (silently or a loud) and you will release lots of stress you have held within.

If you don't believe and won't give prayer a chance, ask friends or family you know who do, and I am certain the prayers will flow freely for your healing.

I was alone much of the time when mama died, as none of my family lived close, and my husband was traveling across country because of his job.

Fortunately with the recent passing of my twin, my husband is no longer on the road.

He and Jesus keep me stabilized, though the flood gates have been open more than shut since Morris' death.

It has brought thoughts of my parents, my sister and her husband, and now my twin, to the forefront of my mind. All the years of my life my family of five have been so important to me. They are firmly planted in my heart and mind.

Writing for me is the best diversion from the reality of it all....at least temporarily. I am not afraid, just feel so strange at this time.

If you are alone or away from family and friends, pick up a newspaper or a telephone. Get on the Internet.

Often times you will locate organizations made up of participants who are going through the same stressors you are trying to diminish.

There are trained leaders who are helpful in guiding you through the toughest of times, and many are on line.

If you join a group of folks, you may hear similar scenarios that give you more understanding, and perhaps, new friendships along the way!

As human beings most of us have the beautiful quality of wanting to help those who are in any type of need.

It may take a bit of research to find what you are looking for, a bit of courage to make that initial call, but it will expedite the matter of healing. You may even find new doors in the area of spiritual realms open for you to explore.

Would you suggest to someone you love getting help if needed? You would. Give yourself a push and then a big hug!

In making an important decision one time, my daughter told me she felt like God had literally kicked her in the fanny to change her situation. She did, and it was the right thing to do.

Write your feelings on paper and then read what you have written.

Let your feelings surface. Sometimes we find by doing this practice, we are in denial; we don't even realize what we are feeling.

If you aren't the type person who communicates easily with others, it would be beneficial to write your feelings in a journal.

As a writer I know that when words are released from my head to the paper, I am able to review my thoughts and gain a more rounded perspective of them.

Often writing is the greatest relief you will find. You do not have to be an author to write. Do not write with a critical eye towards spelling, punctuation, and so forth.

This is to get your feelings out on paper. Sometimes just reading thoughts again will help with that perspective.

I recall after Mama's death hearing a song or seeing something that reminded me of her. It would trigger a river of tears initially. There would be no advance warning. Be patient with yourself. You have a right to cry, and if you need to do so, just do it. Keep in mind these outbursts will not last forever. I promise.

I also found myself at times riddled with guilt for what I do not do for Mama, and also for complaining to others (towards the end) about how tired I was, and how this care giving changed my life. For heaven's sake – Mama was DYING! I was angry with myself for missed opportunities and big mistakes. There were many instances I could have done just the smallest of things and really made her life a bit better.

Guess what? I am human, just like you. I was not an experienced caregiver. I never watched someone whither on the vine and painfully die. I did the best I could with the knowledge I knew to be true at the timeCut yourself a bit of slack in this area.

No matter how often you kick yourself in the fanny, or how you feel remorse, you can never go back. You can never change the past. All you can do is use and share the knowledge you gained, and work to heal yourself so you can make the rest of your life full. Those in the circle of your life will appreciate your efforts.

Think about it. No matter what we did or did not do, no matter how much we love another person, we cannot control his or her life. We cannot prevent "time and unforeseen circumstance" (as the Bible says) from happening to those we love. We cannot stop the inevitable, nor wind the clock backwards.

In reflection I realize that no matter how guilty I felt initially, no matter how angry I was at myself, my motives were never bad towards Mama. I was selfish and impatient sometimes, but I tried never to reflect these feelings to her. She felt guilty enough needing my help. She never wanted to be a burden to anyone.

I am still realizing lessons I learned throughout it all. They still will enhance the remainder of my life if I can simply put the knowledge to work. There is not an elderly person that passes within my vision that I do not have a greater concern and compassion for because of what I learned from Mama's passing.

Yearly holidays, birthdays, anniversaries, and family gatherings may remind you how much you miss your loved one. They may trigger those old feelings of sadness. Be patient. If you were exceptionally close to your mama, as I was, grieving may last longer than you would expect. I talked to Mama or saw her every day for ten years. That was a great loss for me.

Be patient with others too as sometimes they may feel awkward in knowing what to say or do. My daughter called me on a regular basis during those first few months after Mama died. We only touched briefly on Mama's passing.

After a while I admitted to Fawn I did not speak much about Mama because it was painful, and I tried to block it out of my mind. That made me feel terribly guilty, as I thought I was forgetting her. To my surprise, Fawn confessed she had been doing the same thing and we shared the same feelings.

We came to the conclusion neither of us was wrong. Our love for Mama had not lessened. We had simply found a way to cope. As we spoke, more and more we began to talk about the wonderful times we had with Mama. We spoke of her sense of humor, her consistent love for all the family, and the way she would whistle a tune and make us all smile.

We began to bring the Spirit of her love back, and the grief lessened while precious memories came into our hearts.

When you face these mountains of emotion remember a few practical suggestions. Emotions can wear you down physically and mentally. So please try to get enough rest and nourishment for your body. We are truly combination of mind, body and spirit, and when all are in sync our emotions are more under our control.

Be careful not to use medications or alcohol to cope with grief. Those things are temporary fixes, and they can become a problem worse than battling grief.

Get back into a regular routine as soon as possible and it will be very good for you. The structure of returning to a normal routine can be very therapeutic.

Also if possible postpone major decisions until you are thinking calmly and a little more with intellect than emotion.

As this chapter comes to an end you are probably wondering where does the triumph (in the title of the chapter) come in?

Webster's Dictionary defines triumph as follows: "Victory is success, gaining of superiority in any contest, to rejoice in...." Perhaps that does not seem applicable for the moment, however I will explain.

For Christian's the tragedy came when our Lord was crucified. The triumph came at His resurrection.

If you are a person who has hope in the Lord's grace and promise, then you must keep vigil. Remember there will be a resurrection of your mama and, all of us who are believers.

Though your kinship with your mama will be placed on hold for now, the hope of your eternal resurrection must be kept in the forefront of your mind.

You must also recognize the resurrection of your ability to persevere in the challenges of your life.

With your growth you may touch the heart of someone in a similar situation. You must ask for the strength move onward and upward in this life, and to fulfill your mission on this planet earth

I know from personal experience that the Lord is close to the brokenhearted and saves those who are crushed in spirit.

Keep a positive attitude. You will be a great example for others.

Be tenacious. Keep trying. We all have losses. No one can fully appreciate the heart wrenching feeling each of us has to endure.

I do not understand the pain others must endure, but I will find room in my heart to have great understanding for the losses of others too.

Use the gifts you have been given. Be compassionate and look to the Lord for the values He taught us. You can love without question and stop thinking that your lot in life is far harder than that of others. We all bare our own cross. We cannot know another person's burdens. We cannot change the days of our lives.

We can however, always use our gift of choice, and endeavor to make the right choices - which will in turn - help direct our paths.

Lastly, do not underestimate the value of praising God, as you know Him, and the power of prayer. Miracles happen every day.

If you do not believe in these things, you might just give God an earshot of praise and prayer silently. It certainly cannot hurt. The worst that can happen is nothing changes. The best that can happen is you will find new life and miracles and power of prayer. Take a chance. It will be worth the effort, I promise.

"Cast thy burden upon the Lord, and He shall sustain thee:

He shall never suffer the righteous to be moved."

                        Psalm 55:22

"God is our refuge and strength, a very present help in trouble."

                        Psalm 46:1

"Blessed are they that mourn; for they shall be comforted."

                        Matthew 5:4

Mama 80, and Dillon 11

Beloved by Everyone all
Mama a tiny little woman, under five feet tall.
Dillion a large dog, over 100 pounds.

Both gentle with giant hearts!

Chapter 11

Chapter 11

Reflections

I never knew what changes the loss of my mother would bring to my life. It is not as if someone can look at me and say, "Oh look, she is different. Her mother died." I am recognizing truths I have known before, but now I want to live them and reflect them, not just be cognizant of the presence of them. Suddenly I realize I am embracing every moment with new ideas and new joyous moments.

The lives we have been given pass quickly and we gain wisdom as we follow our paths. Be persistent and keep searching. Be happy and love one another.

When your Mama passes, you may not feel that one door has closed and another has opened, as the saying goes.

It may feel as if someone slammed a door in your face and then asked you what you will do now? It can be a shock and you may not feel you are able to recover. You will survive.

I guarantee if you stay flexible in life and keep a positive attitude, no matter what challenge you face your life will begin to take new form.

Your path will become clearer and you will open your eyes and heart to what life now, in the present.

Try to anticipate and be curious. Drop the words dread and fear from your vocabulary. For most of us what we fear in life never comes to fruition so it is a waste of the life to be afraid of the future.

Satan would love to have us fearful of what is to come. Never doubt our Creator, nor the power He bestows upon us to be able to handle effectively whatever trials are laid upon us.

None of us will fully understand now what this life is all about and why things that seem so terrible have to happen. Only God knows, but often we wonder…Why?

It is because we are only finite, trying to coexist with the intelligence of God in appraising each situation. It cannot happen. It must be then that faith must step in and take over our insecurities.

There is a healing when dealing with the loss of a loved one that must take place. Time, understanding, energy, and daily work mustering through the steps of grief will vary with each person. As I mentioned previously there are proven emotional healings that must be accomplished before you can totally move forward.

A step towards healing that will take time and energy must be done daily. Practice allowing yourself a certain amount of time for grief and sorrow, and then switch your emotions to your intellect to rise above getting into the habit of being sorrowful every day. We are creatures of habit.

You must work to subdue sorrow and elevate your thoughts to carry you from where you are to where you want to be. Work to remember all the wonderful memories and experiences you were able to share with your mama.

Work with your newly gained knowledge about aging to help yourself as you begin to age. Help and share with others. Step by step, with a little support and positive thoughts and prayers, you will begin to celebrate life once again.

Incorporate the techniques I have mentioned previously in this book. You may not need to use everything but you'll have a starting point You might even consider mentioning to this person that you are a new caregiver and you want her to work with you so you both will. You may need to create specific tips for your specific scenario.

Trust your thoughts and your intellect. Consider this caregiving you are doing as a learning process for both you and the person receiving your care. Enjoy wonderful days. Make her a part of your endeavors and suggest she will probably be teaching you some things too.

Beyond these basic hints to make life easier, give your mama just as much love and consideration as possible. Don't forget lots of hugs. Hugs are healing!

As children we jump and run never thinking about own futures. We slam our bodies into the ground and each other.

Some of us fill our partially developed bodies with excesses of candy and ice cream, pushing our vegetables aside. In our youth many of us get little sleep and seem to love to party.

As adults we carelessly eat and drink whatever we choose, and we rarely think about the effects these things are having on this body we live in!

Think of it. This body is our place to live. This body is a holy tabernacle.

Few of us follow the rules managing the body's health systems. How many times this week did you take in specific breaths of oxygen to invigorate or relax yourself? Have you exercised at all? What about water?

It is the most important ingredient, next to oxygen and yet many of us never drink a glass of it.

Have you had a balanced meal today? Get the point?

We are "mind, body and spirit" combined into one, and if we want to meld our intellect with our emotion, and find stability and optimal health, we must keep our bodies healthy.

You can expect the body as it ages, to deteriorate from what we do to it. It is the natural way of things. Like a blossom on a rose bush there is a beginning and the fruition of a beautiful bud opening into a fragrant flower.

There is that time the rose opens fully to the warming rays of the sun.

There is a time it will begin to wilt and lose its vibrant color and fragrance. We expect this to happen. And, so it is with human kind on earth, but many people are even afraid to consider aging and death. Do not be afraid. It is natural and it happens to us all.

Be very careful if your mama is told she must have any surgery. We expect things to go wrong on occasion, but thoroughly check into the necessity before letting her have a procedure.

Mama was old school. As a child she was taught that physicians were almost gods. Be aware of this scenario.

Recently I trusted that physicians and the

local ER were caring for me.

I wound up with permanent disabilities and it was TOTALLY unnecessary. The slipshod and negligent treatment of me now plays a major role in the rest of my life. My problem could have been corrected within a couple of days.

Do not simply trust the physicians and medical staffs. Get second opinions. Research what they are suggesting. Always get copies of any tests and also the doctor's note after a visit. You absolutely have a right to them.

Do this for your mama too. It may save her life, or ease her burden, as the days grow shorter.

As we grower older, we take longer to heal from an illness or surgery. Though some surgeries are really necessary, others may not be so important if you really take time to evaluate the results. There are no guarantees when it comes to surgery.

Mama was advised to have a foot surgery. The podiatrist named the problem. It was a Morton's neuroma. Mama's foot had been very painful and it was almost impossible to put a shoe on.

Every time she took a step, the ball of her foot hurt so badly, she just felt she could not handle the pain any longer.

The podiatrist told her it would take a while to heal, but would really help. In Mama's case, her foot took three or four months to heal and even then, it never took the pain completely away.

She was unable to be independent for a long while and she was bitterly disappointed with the results.

Her foot pain was a continual problem that never ceased to make her wish she had never opted for surgery.

The second surgery was one that many seniors opt to have and most often it is successful.

Mama had been through hip replacement surgeries before and was not the least frightened of the surgery.

She knew the recovery period would be lengthy and that it would come in increments.

After the surgery she had to stay in a specialty hospital where physical therapists worked with her and helped her slowly regain her strength and agility.

I believe the surgeon did an excellent job with the hip replacement. That was not the problem I am going to mention.

The problem, and I believe this with all my heart, was that Mama had severe osteoporosis. The surgeon (and he was qualified) did not take this into account. He was not an expert in osteoporosis

After the surgery Mama screamed over and over again, "My back, my back!" she screamed as she wreathed in pain and tried to reach her low back. She moaned in excruciating pain and her head tossed from side to side. She pushed our hands away and again attempted to grope her back.

It was horrifying to see her in that kind of pain. My husband and I were distraught and because there simply no way to console her.

She remained in critical pain for hours. Eventually the new hip was fine and she was mobile, but her back never got improved. I believe the damage done to her bones in the surgery really shortened her life.

Prior to the surgery the anesthesiologist had found it difficult, for some unknown reason, to give Mama the shot she needed to put her out for the surgery.

She told me later he had tried six times to give her the shot – unsuccessfully. On the seventh it worked.

During the surgery it was necessary for her to be lying flat on her back.

When she was awake it was impossible for her to straighten her back because the bones were weak and bent with osteoporosis.

I believe when she was "out" for the surgery and when they placed her on the gurney her back straightened because it was forced to do so.

Her weight of her body pressed her porous and bent bones straight for those hours. Therein I believe it further weakened the bones.

When up and walking she could never straighten her back and it seemed to be worse. I think that the straightening of bones already bent from wear and tear did additional damage to her skeleton.

She saw a domino effect of that damage in days and months to come. It weakened her skeleton.

I wondered if I had known about how the surgery was done, if I had spoken with the doctor and explained about her osteoporosis, if there had been another way, perhaps the outcome would have been different. This was another instance I learned but I fear it was to the detriment of my Mama.

When Mama died the doctor really never knew why she died, though he believed her spine had collapsed abruptly when she sat up. It made sense to me as she had broken those ribs before going to the hospital, and when she came out it was the other side that was painful.

I do not know how I could have changed the hip scenario. She was having terrible pain walking. Perhaps if I had known to bring up the osteoporosis to the doctor something could have been done!

A method by which the hip now can be replaced is so much easier and faster to recover from. It is called the anterior hip replacement. I never even had to go to rehabilitation to use my hip. I was up the next day. This approach is minimally invasive.

Jumping forward to the present time keep in mind, one in two women WILL have osteoporosis. One in four men WILL have it as well. Osteoporosis is serious. Make sure you have regular bone density scans.

Do not take Boniva. I was told after taking it for seven years it does not build bone. It hardens them. During that time I had a broken leg, three broken wrists, and a broken back. It never occurred to me the drug was probably making my bones snap. I trusted the doctor's recommendation. Oh snap!

Medications are another area to be very careful. Be aware that most medications are constipating, particularly Norco, Oxycotin, Percocet, and Morphine, and similar drugs. It is challenging for most seniors to have regular bowels. Poor habits in drinking too little water and an improper diet also take a toll.

Mama used to tell me she was sick of everything. She never however, tired of candy and popcorn with loads of butter. I think she was just tired of cooking and eating alone, in order to eat nutritiously. It was difficult for her to stand long enough to really cook a meal.

Another problem seniors face with constipation is not being able (or choosing to) exercise to get the metabolism moving.

Physical disabilities may also keep your Mama from using the bathroom when she needs to go, and then the urge may pass, leading to constipation.

Mama rubbed her little tummy and told me she had taken stool softness with her pain pills, but she was still constipated. That was a problem I could relate to for sure (the constipation) – but not constipation to the extreme she was living.

The colon is an important organ and the way for the body to rid waste material that is no longer needed and is supposed to the body. Constipation can lead to other infirmities.

Even though I was familiar with colon cleansing for some reason it NEVER occurred to me to take Mama to make sure she was in good shape and not nearing a fecal impact. I believe getting Mama colonics as I do regularly now, might have REALLY made her life more comfortable and actually kept her more physically in tune!

That was another of those "Hind sight is twenty-twenty moments," I wish I could have changed. Pain pills are so constipating, but when you have a real need for them, they are life-saving!

I know now there is a prescription you can get to counteract the constipating effects of pain meds. I know – pills, pills, pills – however, there comes a real time of need for so many folks, and then they are a blessing.

Weigh the value of medications against the potential reaction your Mama may have when she takes the medicine. There are many home remedies that are effective for colds and such. A course of antibiotics in some cases are necessary. Be sure if your Mama begins a prescription of antibiotics that she finishes it all.

I have my doubts about the majority of prescription drugs you see advertised on television and/ or the internet or radio there days.

Have you ever actually listened the reactions taking many medications can cause – heart attack, even death! The warnings are worse that the purposed good the prescriptions are supposed to take.

"Take these but be aware," (then beautiful, happy and healthy people are shown, with lovely music) as they flash on the screen, "You can get several kinds of cancers, if your moods get violent contact someone, these pills can kill you, etc. etc. etc."

Terrifying and yet, the relieve of overwhelming pain is worth the risk.

I would NEVER have gotten the vaccinations for Covid 19 had it not be required for me to have entry to the hospital and an urgent surgery. I honestly believe mind over matter and our natural immunity can do more, with less consequences. I made the mistake of following up with a booster, and I could hardly lift my arm for a week…also, I felt kind of sick for a few days too.

If you haven't gotten the shots, my advice is not to do so. Each person has the choice of what to do – thus far!

What really gets me with the covid fear rush to get vaccines is NO ONE on planet earth knows what the long term effects will be.

Now those IIC's (Idiots in charge) want to immunize babies and small children.

These precious little human beings are not even in danger! I am absolutely against vaccinating children and babies. There

As we watch all who are involved with the prescription tidal waves, millionaires grow, and some citizens are dying. I believe not from this illness, but from poverty, pre-existing weaknesses, and lack of care, and even from reactions not reported by media.

Many deaths listed as Covid deaths were simply signed off that way for hospitals to make money.

If they tested positive, whether the disease killed them or not, that always wound up being listed as the cause of death. More money! But this is another story.

Seniors over the age of sixty-five have a stronger version of the flu vaccine now, and I do believe getting vaccinated, and also getting the pneumonia shot is very important.

I know there has been the train of thought that vaccines are not good, however in countries where they are not available many diseases run rampant. You cannot get the flu from getting a flu shot as it is not a live virus. One medicine I had heard horror stories about was morphine.

It was always a medication I assumed would dope a person into a euphoric state and a person could become addicted. I was right in both assumptions but I learned there is also great value in using morphine for certain medical cases.

When Mama began a regime of a low dose of morphine, she was in a wheelchair, and it was very difficult for her to walk on her own, without it. She was very shy about taking it and I found weeks after it was prescribed, she had been "saving it" for a real emergency. That did not help!

I felt "walking and managing her horrible pain" was real enough!

Once Mama got used to the slightly euphoric sense morphine gives a person, she began to feel better. She told me the pain was still there however somehow it did not bother her as much. After a few weeks she was again using her cane and able to walk around a bit. I did most of the driving so I was not concerned about that aspect.

I am not endorsing this for everyone. It should be a last resort for those who are in critical pain and really have need of it.

I am taking Oxycodone currently because recently I had a fall and terrible experience. I was forced to have two surgeries.

I do feel nauseated if I do not eat with the medication and it is indeed, very constipating. I do not feel a "high" as my pain is over-whelming.

These medications can be addictive so it is important, when you or your Mama can, to wean yourself off of the narcotic drugs.

Mama was not able to do so, but she did not take huge amounts for a high….she needed the medication for living a decent latter part of her life. I was grateful for that.

Never stop abruptly, but only under the doctor's direction.

I asked my doctor if I am addicted, though I knew I am not, as I take two a day, three if the pain is severe.. She said since I have weaned off most of the drugs, and do have great pain, she feels I am not addicted, but using the drug to manage the pain.

One experimental medication Mama chose to try actually caused her to have a heart attack. It was some radical treatment for osteoporosis. Mama was supposed to give herself a shot in the tummy every day. Believe me, after that first shot we never went that route again.

There is a medication that has been available for twenty-five years or more. A single shot in the tummy every day. I don't know if it is the same medication or not, but I opted not to take it because it caused osteosarcoma in rats! I will not take a medication with a possibility of causing cancer in my bones.

Do your homework for you and your mama.

My little Mama was so strong. She just grabbed her heart, refused to go to the hospital, and began breathing slowly. Even the nurse who was there to assist, if necessary, could not believe the mental power of Mama. Be very selective and inquisitive about these things for your mama.

The wrong medicine and unnecessary surgeries can diminish the quality of the last years of her life, if you are not cautious.

Do not treat her like a baby, but as an equal. There are exceptions to every rule. Dementia and Alzheimer's disease are cause to rethink that last statement.

Check information and discuss the positive and negative results that may occur.

If you feel strongly against something, calmly tell her why. She will most likely respond by listening. It is when an elderly person is treated like an ignorant child that they will balk at your thoughts and suggestions.

In all honesty, wouldn't you?

Also keep in mind your Mama is from an entirely different generation than yours, and her ways may differ from yours. That does not necessarily mean she is wrong. She may simply have a different perspective of the scenario. Work together.

If your Mama has dementia or Alzheimer's disease that is an entirely different situation. You must be assertive (with love) and with ongoing education and entirely different methods.

Discuss things with your Mama if she is open to discussion.

If she isn't, then think of ways to open conversations with positive thoughts about each scenario. Perhaps you can ask her a question and if she has any ideas regarding the subject. She wants to be a part of what is happening in her life.

Make sure you do your homework if you disagree and then you
can back your position with facts that will direct her towards her own safety and health. The bottom line if you are at an impasse is to remind her you DO NOT HAVE TO HELP HER!

The harsh reality of this may help snap her into a workable mold. It certainly did my little Mama. She mellowed out right away.

I said it with love, but firmly.

If I could change one thing as I reflect upon days past, it would be the decision, at Mama's request, not to spend the night at her house the night before she died. I had considered staying but she insisted I go home.

Michael was headed home and because she was really a sweet, she knew it would be good for me to meet him there. She only asked that I be sure to come over to help her balance her checkbook in the morning. I would certainly do that.

I walked with her into her bedroom and she sat on the bed. and then got in between the sheets. I gently tucked her in.

She had been darling during the day. Even with her terrible pain she kept a smile on her face most of the afternoon. Near bedtime it seemed her pain had diminished to almost nothing and she was cheerful and talkative. I had no idea it would be the last day she would spend with me.

After her death I frequently felt guilty about not staying with her. She had died alone. My husband, Michael swears it was a blessing, and happened exactly the way it was supposed to happen.

He said I had done everything I could by being with Mama when she was alive. He thought mama would not have wanted me to be there when she died.

Michael said I had given her all I could give, and that she was not alone, but with her Maker. He told me not to have regrets. God was with her all along – at the beginning – and at the end of her life. Mama used to tell me we are born alone and we die alone, except for the presence of God, who is with us at all times.

Each parent is different. We are all different. There are common denominators though that keep us in touch and connected. We all come in as infants and hopefully, we will all leave after living our lives.

We all have a particularly wonderful gift, and that is the gift of choice!

No matter what happens in our lives we have the free will to respond any way we choose. We make choices one hundred percent of the time. Each movement is a choice. Sometimes our choices depend somewhat on the scenarios.

Sometimes our choices will drop us into the pit of hell, or take us to the edge of heaven, but no matter what the majority of us have no choice of how and when we will die.

When your Mama dies it will be up to you to CHOOSE what happens next. Give yourself time to mourn, time to calm down, and time to get back to a regular schedule before those bigger choices are made.

For almost two years I was inconsolable at times. Maybe it was because we were best friends. Maybe it was because Mama was my most adoring fan and her death left me with a void in my life for a time. Perhaps I felt inside that life would never be the same again.

I wasn't even able to being this book for years after, as every time I started, tears would manifest, and I just couldn't.

Then one day I remembered Mama told me one time:

"The only things you can be sure of baby are God, my love, and change! So it was important to focus your life on the fact that everything changes! Be flexible if you plan to survive successfully."

She was so totally right. In the snap of your fingers your life can do a three-hundred-and-sixty-degree turn.

I think at one time I believed there was a proper time to mourn, and if I began to celebrate life again, it would show a lack of love and concern for the loss of Mama. I was surely wrong about that. The proper time to mourn depends of the people and the scenario. It is totally individual.

Remember life is brief. Mama said, "When I die you can mourn my loss but don't get caught up in it and make it a career. Get on to other things and be happy!" She was absolutely right about that too.

It seems like yesterday she was gone, but it has been over twenty-five years. Now people may look at me and think I am a senior citizen. They probably do already, and that is alright, as they would be right! ☺ I try not to dwell on it! Better to age than the other option!

It is a blessing for those of you who know the truth. If however you are unsure of life after death or unable to call upon a god for help, then use you intellect to begin to rise above your sorrow.

Step just far enough away from your emotion to meld your emotions with your intellect. You can do it. I've mentioned this before. Keep an open mind, as you never know when God may speak to you. What a wonderful surprise that would be!

Your world will never be exactly the same. That does not necessarily mean it will be worse. You will learn hidden lessons and gain wisdom.

You will learn during a major life change, how to handle it, and you can be an example for all those around you.

Life may blossom into an even more complete and beautiful thing. I loved the James Allen Book, "As a Man Thinketh." A short quote from it contains wonderful truths.

"All that a man achieves and all that he fails to achieve is the direct result of his own thoughts."

"In a justly ordered universe, where loss of equipoise would mean total destruction individual responsibility must be absolute. A man's weakness and strength, purity and impurity, are his own, and not another man's; they are brought about by himself, and not by another; and they can only be altered by himself, never by another."

"His condition is also his own, and not another mans. His suffering and his happiness are evolved from within. As he thinks, so he is; as he continues to think, so he remains."

My sweet Lynn, my sister-in-law, sent these lovely words to me years ago. I do not know the author for certain but it does sound like another James Allen quotation to me.

"We are what we think.
All that we are arises with our thoughts.
With our thoughts we make the world.
Speak or act with an impure mind
And trouble will follow you.
As the wheel follows the ox that draws the cart, we are what we think."

<u>All that we are arises with our thoughts.</u>

<u>With our thoughts we make the world.</u>

<u>Speak or act with a pure mind and</u>

<u>happiness will follow you</u>

<u>As your shadow, unshakable."</u>

In the end, suffering is always the effect of

wrong thought in some direction.

Suffering is necessary sometimes in this life,

but be not self-indulgent in your mourning.

Consider the true effect you have upon

yourself, and also upon others.

Chapter 12

Chapter 12

Legacy of Love

Webster's Dictionary defines legacy as something handed down to a successor or bequeathed to an individual; anything left by a will. I chose the word legacy. It seems quite appropriate to include in the title of this chapter.

I will share with you a small portion of the legacy of love Mama left our family and anyone's heart who was fortunate enough to know her. I was sure before Mama passed away that her love would live on.

I was not surprised by the number of ways Mama's legacy of love still resounds in the lives of all who shared her time on this planet. When your mama transcends our time and space, it will help to know that there may be many ways in which she will always be with you, and perhaps, for generations to come.

In our elderly if we can STOP TO TAKE THE TIME, WHEN WE STOP AND TAKE THE TIME, we see the past living in our present.

Their history and experience may just possibly be a primary factor in our extended education in life. We may all dream of our future. MAKE the time to listen to those who have already experienced at least a portion of what we may be going through right now.

Listen to the past. Listen to how your parent grew with different experiences, in a different time. You may laugh. You may cry. You may be amazed at what you hear. I know I was!

Our specific experiences may be different, but we all have human emotions and needs. If your parent is still around you take time to really hear what he or she may have to say.

So many truisms have come to light since Mama's death. I wish I could sit across from her and listen just one more time!

Mama taught me courage. In the face of the biggest challenges in life, we may question our faith. We will face growing aches and pains, a loss of earthly dreams, our world shrinking, and ultimately death. She taught me not by just saying that you have to be tough. She was tough. She was a LIVING example of the right things to do. It was an honor to watch and learn from her.

Suicide was in Mama's mind for a time. She even bought the book Final Exit, hoping to find a way out if the path became unbearable.

I think she knew she could never resort to suicide. "We are not supposed to kill." she would say. "That means not even ourselves, as much as sometimes, I would like a way out."

She told me that if she committed suicide, she would be a poor example of true courage. She wanted to teach her children and grandchildren even in the most difficult areas of life.

She was a hero to me for such high-minded courage in the face of insurmountable challenges.

Though our search to know more about osteoporosis she taught me when a problem arises not to give up hope.

Research, talk to people, go to great lengths to resolve any problem. Our search was to find what could help ease her pain. It was too late in the disease for Mama to be cured. Her mind found peace as soon as she knew what she was dealing with as far as prognosis.

I will never have the problem to the degree she did because today much more is known about osteoporosis, and there are medical research results that have given people options to live longer and healthier lives, even with osteoporosis.

Mama taught me that there are actually

many gifts that come with aging. Rewards of aging you might ask. What can they be?

We do develop patience as we age. Even those will totally impatient personalities will find their tolerance blossoming.

Tempers modify. There simply is not a reason good enough to be angry when you realize you have so little time left to live, and no guarantee of even a few years in good health, is offered to anyone.

You begin to care a lot less what other people think of what you do, say, or dress like!

You can pretty much say anything you like when you become a senior citizen. Some people will look at you with distain and impatience at your slowness anyway – so why not?

I have to chuckle as I write this one. I remember how Mama used to flirt with the clerks at the store. She would tell them, "You are awfully handsome. I can say that because I am old and I have earned the right to say anything I want." They always seemed to enjoy seeing her and most often they gave her a hug.

When you become a senior citizen. Some Major changes will find you perhaps, somewhat unwilling to give up those things that Gave you freedom as an adult; driving and Such.

As you age your need to do something all the time diminishes, as does your ability to keep going hour after hour.

You truly can find satisfaction in rest, reading, and simply in quiet moments. Because your time as an elderly person is limited, you learn to revere each moment in time.

Mama even said her prayers had changed. She learned to say thank you more often than asking for things. Her prayers evolved into appreciation for each moment.

If you have grandchildren who spend time with you it will be precious time.

They will appreciate their grandma and will keep you current as to what is happening in the world of the young people.

There are more gifts and rewards as you age and they will come to light for you in due time. Pay attention. The pressure is off as far as beauty verses comfort; comfort will always win.

There will be a time you just do not feel the pressure to compete, but just enjoy being yourself with no race to be competitive for anything!

A realization that much of these feelings were brought to light by advertisers trying to sell beauty products or the coolest vehicles, or biggest house; the realization will settle in and free you!

During the prime of life (many consider this time to be twenty to forty years old), you are so busy trying to whip life that life ends up whipping you. Take time to stop and REALLY smell the roses.

As silly as it sounds part of Mama's legacy was the way she did things.

We have all heard, "Oh my gosh, I have become my mother!" I remember thinking that. But now I realize that that is not all bad!

It can be very good if you are lucky enough to have a good mother. Do not misunderstand. All parents make mistakes.

I made plenty of them myself. But if your mother raised you with a home full of love, those mistakes diminish with time, and the love remains.

Mama used to tell me, when I was in the midst of raising three children, "Do not walk from one room to another without your arms full; something in hand to transport, part of a task to accomplish.

Always double bag your trashcans, and empty your trash cans every day.

Use your leftovers. Be creative and you can decrease your food bill. Never waste anything.

Let your children join in when you are cooking or cleaning. It may take longer, but it will benefit them and you.

The time together is brief and in years to come you will be grateful for those moments spent together."

I listened. I did not always let her know, and it may have taken a long while for me to learn her techniques, but I can proudly say, I am like my Mama. She was a peach.

During much of the down time, time that she was healing or ill, we talked. There was a point I thought I would NEVER be interested in politics. She had an incessant interest in politics. I find these days, at least up until the past three or four years, my interest peeked.

I wanted to know as a citizen, what is happening. I wanted to be sure my rights as imparted in the Constitution were not being breeched.

I am afraid, lately I feel big brother has already claimed his domain in the United States.

Because we are a melting post of cultures and peoples, it would be almost impossible for citizens to fight where the government is headed. We have the vote but I believe it means little. It is the money that brings our nominees to elections.

You have to be rich to be a leader in our time – or you have to have BIG money and have media behind you. Besides those with the biggest guns will always rule. That is a totally different conversation, and that is for sure.

We may be limited in our rights these days but we always have the right to believe in our hearts and pray every day. Those are powerful gifts we have.

The things I miss the most about Mama are those things I am trying to LIVE in my lifetime. She taught me about unconditional love and forgiveness. She taught me praise if honest is better than being critical.

She taught me not to judge others but instead to have compassion and understanding. She taught me to honor the rights of others to make different choices.

Think about these things and try to stop longer and see the vast horizon the years of your Mama's life can open to you, if only you pay attention. It will not always be easy because often you have to squeeze in a hundred things you ordinarily do not have to do, and you will be probably be exhausted most of the time.

Mama taught all my clan and many other folks she crossed paths with values that would enhance their own families, and improve the quality of their lives.

She accepted each of us for who we were as human beings. Though we were as diverse in personalities and careers as we were in spiritual matters.

She told me no matter what if you look for something good in each person; you can always find at least one attribute.

We easily judge (or misjudge) people and often we are way out of line. Besides we are not supposed to judge one another. That is out of our hands.

She was quite frank on a personal level with each of us when she could see we needed some help. She never forced us to act upon her suggestions; she simply kindly tried to help. She always did it on a private basis, never including everyone in on anyone else's personal business.

She offered some enlightenment and wisdom to each of us. Everyone in the family respected Mama nd considered her the matriarch.

When Mama considered something "life-threatening", she became ten feet tall and mightier than a warrior.

All aspects of relationship and life problems seem to have been covered during her time. with me.

I did jot down a few quotes Mama said those last couple of years. I think they are part of her legacy of love and worth sharing.

"Age is only the number of years you have lived in your body. It is another area for people to be prejudice, and they had better get over it, because we all age if we live long enough!"

"The devil is in the details. He can manifest in your words. Words need to be thought about and carefully so before being said out loud. Once words are spoken, they are alive and the damage is done."

"Women learn to live with things. They do not need to complain about it all. Much is kept undercover."

"The challenges women face simply make them stronger and more resilient."

"Old people can be fuddy-duddies. They talk like they are covered with mildew. Do not let this happen to you. Do not let your heart harden or the devil wins."

"Keep a happy face if you can, even if you do not mean it one hundred percent. Eventually you will be happier."

"Forever is composed of now."

"The most difficult and the most rewarding job in the world is parenting."

"Love your life. It is the only choice. If you cannot love it do what you can to change it."

"It is important to talk about death. It is the natural progression of things. I have never been afraid of dying. It is the living that is tough."

"Bored people are boring people."

"I am in a large part, who I am because I was fortunate to have the backing of a wonderful man for forty-five years. He was such a great love and never judged me. I need to live up to his expectations of me. "

"Never take ANY LOVE for granted."

"The only thing in the world that counts is love."

"Money and possessions come and go, and so do human beings, but the human being is the most valuable of all.

She told me that the love money REALLY is the root of all evil."

"Do not turn off a conversation with a fellow human for a radio show, television show, or a movie."

"Children are a gift from God and they are to be treasured."

"If you lose your sense of humor along the way, you lose your life."

"If you use the Bible as a guide for your life you will never lose your way. It was written by the hands of men, but God inspired it, and the messages given to us are urgent to live the best life possible. All subjects are covered in the Bible, and the more you read, the more clarity in meaning will come to you!"

Even if it seems difficult at times you continue to read it, you will eventually understand even what seems confusing or mysterious at first, and you will be blessed. Be persistent."

"If you can count your <u>true friends</u> on one hand when you are old you have been blessed."

"Never abuse children, either physically, or verbally. It will stay with them for life. I did not say to withhold a planned swat on the fanny to get their attention. Spare the rod and spoil the child."

"LOVE means sacrifice. Jesus sacrificed for love."

I wish I had jotted down more of Mama's wisdom and humor. She was hysterically funny as long as I can remember.

The only time she had to dig for her wit was when she was overwhelmed with pain.

Mama said that sometimes life is difficult and sometimes it is a pleasure. One of the most wonderful attributes I saw in Mama was that she never gave up hope. She would climb whatever stumbling block was placed in her way, or kick it out of the way with attitude!

Whatever gave a negative experience to her, she would find the wisdom, and move forward to the next challenge.

I have only touched lightly on her legacy of love. Many gifts were left to us that are incorporated into each of our daily lives. They remain alive and will be in our hearts forever.

Your parent may have much to offer if you simply listen and say, "Share with me special things about your life. Things no other person may know…experiences and such."

She told me that the things we pay attention to, the things we listen to, the things we study, and the things we think, will create our lives. We can always choose our way.

She left a few hand-written gems in her paper box, and I would like to share these.

"Technology may be the ruination of man. As humans we have not advanced enough to even master the most common of emotions such as anger, hatred, sadness, forgiveness, and love."

"Machines will make us stupid, unhealthy and dependent. I don't know why, but I do know this."

"You will never be alone because of God. There is power in the peace of God. There is power in every breath you take. There is power in love."

"Sometimes true love swallows its pride and becomes the gentler soul. There can be no war if you refuse to fight."

"I guess I am still on this earth to serve a purpose, perhaps to be a little light in the darkness. I must serve some purpose for God. We all tend to neglect Him and put all else before Him."

"We tend to forget to say thank you enough to God, and to just praise Him for each moment we have here on earth, our beautiful, though temporary, home."

"We are not here to impress anyone, but to EXPRESS God! Stand up and fight when you are right. You will ALWAYS know in your heart. The small voice from within is God."

"He makes a place for Himself to be filled in each person. Those who find solace in drugs and alcohol and other pastimes are simply trying to fill the void they have because they have not let God reside in His place within each of us. "

"You will find that peace beyond understanding you always hear about, once you open the door and let God in."

"Do not delude your thoughts or try to justify your actions. Do not be insecure about your decisions – in your throbbing heart speak to God as your father and he will speak through you. Let Him speak through your love and actions."

"Give love while you can. No one knows the troubles another person may have seen. That is why we cannot judge another. Help those in need. It could be you in need. Love is mightier than any other emotion on this earth."

"Look upon life as a party. One arrives long after it is started, and one will leave long before it is over. No need to be the life of it and soul of it. Try not to take too much responsibility for it."

"I am not taking everything so personally anymore. I congratulate myself for that."

"I choose to be happy, brave, hopeful, cheerful, cooperative, and accept my own mortality as I see it."

"Our sanity depends essentially on a narrowness of vision. The ability to select the elements vital to survival while ignoring the great truths or avoiding any exposure to reality."

"You will never lose the joy in life if you don't lose your sense of humor. More things are funny than people realize. Take things lightly. What you fret over today won't mean a thing in a few days, it will be easily forgotten."

"Do not let a fight or disagreement turn into a war. If you find laughter you will remember those times with joy. "

"I believe God has a wonderful sense of humor. Don't you think He has a good laugh every time he sees men and women trying to make some sense of one another? Keep it funny!"

"The only things that count in life are the imprints of love that we leave behind us after we are gone."

Mama wrote in her diary a few quotations from various people and authors. I hope they touch you as they did me.

"If you would indeed behold the spirit of death open your heart wide unto the body of life. For life and death are one, even as the river and the sea are one."

"In the depth of your hopes and desires lies your silent knowledge of the beyond and like seeds dreaming beneath the snow your heart dreams of spring."

Gibran

"I have been here since the beginning and I shall be until the end of days. There is no ending to my existence. For the human soul is but a part of a burning torch which God separated from himself at creation. Thus, my soul and your soul are one and we are one with God."

Gibran

"If you would indeed behold the spirit of death open your heart wide unto the body of life. For life and death are one, even as the river and the sea are one."

"Go placidly amidst the noise and the haste, and remember what peace there may be in silence. If you compare yourself to others, you may become vain and bitter: for always there will be greater and lesser persons than yourself. Nurture strength of spirit to shield you in sudden misfortune."

"You are a child of the universe no less than the trees and the stars. You have a right to be here: and whether or not it is clear to you, no doubt the universe is unfolding as it should. Therefore, be at peace be with God, whatever you conceive Him to be. Keep peace within your soul. It is a beautiful world. Strive to be happy."

Max Ehrmann

"Just for today I will try to live through this day only and not tackle my whole life problems at once. I can do something for twelve hours that would appall me if I had to keep it up for a lifetime."

"Just for today I will adjust myself to what is and not try to adjust things to my own desires. I will fit myself to what really is. Just for today I will be unafraid. I especially will be brave and courageous and set a noble example and believe that as I give to the world, so the world will give to me."

                Al-Anon prayer

"There is no medicine like hope, no incentive so great, and no tonic so powerful as expectation of something tomorrow."

                Orison Swett Marden

"When you get into a tight place and everything goes against you so it seems as though you could not hold on a minute longer, never give up, for that is just the place and time that the tide will turn."

Harriet Beecher Stowe

"Art thou in agony?
Then I pray be comforted.
This too shall pass away.
Art thou elated? Be not too gay,
this too shall pass away.
Art thou in danger? Still let reason sway
and cling to hope.
This too shall pass away.
Tempered, art thou? In thee

anguish lay one truth to heart.

This too shall pass away.

What're thou art,

where're thy footsteps stray,

heed these wise words,

This too shall pass away."

Paul Hamilton Hayne

"The day will come when my body will lie upon a white sheet neatly tucked under four corners of a mattress located in a hospital busily occupied with the living and the dying."

At a certain moment a doctor will determine

that my brain has ceased to function and for all practical purposes, my life has stopped."

"When that happens, do not attempt to instill artificial life into my body by the use of a machine, and don't call this my deathbed. Let it be called the Bed of Life, and let whatever is usable be taken from it to help others lead fuller lives. Burn what is left and scatter my ashes to the winds."

"If you must bury something, let it be my faults, my weaknesses and my prejudices against my fellow man. Give my sins to the devil and my spirit to God. If, by chance, you wish to remember me, do it with a kind deed or word to someone who needs you.

"If you do all I have asked, I will live forever."

Robert N. Test

"Be on good terms with hope.
The happiest people you will ever meet are those
who are on good terms with hope.
They are confident that something good
is just around the corner.
Be actively engaged in helping others.
Helping others put us on good terms with hope
because in helping others, we find ourselves"

Marsha J. O'Brien

"Trust your dreams, for in them is hidden gates to eternity. For what is it to die but to stand naked in the wind and to melt into the sun. To cease breathing is to free the breath from its restless tides that it might raise, and expand and seek God unencumbered."

                                Gibran

These were just some of the words Mama lived by and taught in her own life. She was beyond her education, beyond her career, a head of her time, and closer to God than any one of us realized.

She lived a quiet life in her later years, but her love could be heard from state to state and around the world. She was an exceptional Mama, and an exceptional human being. I do not believe she ever knew quite how wonderful she was.

She lives in all our hearts now, and her love, is her legacy. Our spirits will meld again one day.

"Trust in the Lord with all thine heart; and lean not unto thine own understanding."

Proverbs 3:5

"Come to me, all who labor and are heavy laden and I will give you rest. Take my yoke upon you, and learn of me; for I am gentle and lowly in heart: and ye shall find rest unto your souls."

Matthew 11:28-29

"Marvel not at this. The hour is coming, in which all that are in the graves shall hear his voice."

John 5:28

Chapter 13

Chapter 13

Tomorrow

Tomorrow is a tease. It is a time we are sure we are going to see. We can dream of tomorrow, plan for tomorrow, and hope for tomorrow, but it is today we must use as wisely and wonderfully as possible.

The very MOMENT you are finishing this little book is all you have!

Moment by moment we march towards the hope of tomorrow.

I never really dreamed the day would come when Mama would really die. Even with preparations we made together, when she actually passed, I was in a world unknown to me. As surely as new life comes forth each moment, turning into days and years, death will come to us all.

We cannot always be prepared when our loved one dies. In the case of your Mama, particularly if you have not been in a close relationship, it is important to keep in mind that time is fleeting, and old wounds still can be healed.

While writing this book I thought of all of you who have not been as fortunate as I was to have a wonderful and loving Mama.

It is a shame, for whatever circumstances may have caused this, took away special memories and perhaps even a childhood of fun and family.

But while you are still here it is not to late for recovery. While there are moments left in your life and your mama is still here too, find time to mend fences. Why not?

What I have found as I age and watch my peers age, is that we mellow in life about everything.

We have had enough time to feel guilty about our mistakes, enough fights to never want to fight again, and enough loneliness to crave the company our own family. The list of regrets has been reviewed and for the majority of us if we could, would like to do it over again to apply the wisdom we have acquired to our years of living. Alas that is impossible.

What is possible is that with your forgiveness and love, there is still time to register memories that will stay with you until your days are done. Forgiveness is much easier than most people recognize.

Keep in mind that as we grow older, we are not only frail in body, but become highly sensitive to other people's comments and actions. They are still the same person inside, but they live in a body that society deems unpopular, and they face death every single day.

Forgiveness can be simple if you really want to do it. Here is what to do to begin to achieve forgiveness.

Remember how many mistakes you have made and how much you probably regret each one. Would it not be wonderful if you were forgiven for those errors in judgments or choices?

Forget the past. It is the past. It is a done deal! No matter how much a person would like to live the past over, it is impossible. Start anew.

The truth is that when you harbor any feelings that include not forgiving someone, YOU are damaging YOU! To forgive is freeing. Even if you never saw the person again when you forgive someone you grow in character and insight.

It will be a seed you have planted within you that will blossom further, enhancing your own life too. I promise! Keep in mind it is your best option. What are you going to do? Punch your old Mama in the face? Yell and scream at her?

She has plenty to deal with without you adding fuel to the fire.

Take a breath before you pass a judgment. Remember it is impossible to be anyone else's judge! We may attempt to, however, we are really not qualified.

Once you forgive someone it will take you to a higher level in life, and the simple act will begin to make your life better.

It happens the moment you truly forgive someone. You release the negative energy you have been lugging around within you, and leave room for happier moments.

Live today as if this is the only day you have.

It very well may be! We never know what adventure or challenge may await us. I have been blessed to stay positive through the most difficult and painful year of my life this past year. Without a positive attitude and hope I never would have been able to make it.

I also give the most credit to God. He deserves all the credit really. When we are at our weakest, He is at His strongest for us. He has given us tools to help repair our heart and body, and the power of prayer to use and share with others. He never leaves us without help and hope.

Do not waste a moment! It is all we can count on.

This moment is golden…it can be if you CHOOSE it to be.

Take a breath and think before you speak. Once words have been spoken, as Mama said, they are impossible to pull back into our brains. The die is cast. Words become your life. Words can come back to haunt you if not carefully selected.

Practice making the life of the person you are caring for, a task of love. No resentment for the time taken from you own life, no anger for being put in this position. It is almost never the fault of the person who is the one you are caring for; they would much rather not need the help.

This book was written towards caring for your Mama but you can apply the same techniques to any situation of care giving. Man or woman, adult or child, we all need help at some point in our lives. Give cheerfully.

Be honest with yourself. If you feel you are not up to taking the challenge then try to arrange for other help. It will be one hundred percent better for the person to be cared for and also better for you.

Care giving that is filled with resentment or anger will not only destroy the recipient but your tomorrows will truly be filled with regrets and guilt.

If you cannot find help then my first suggestion would be to fall on your knees and ask God to fill your heart with patience, love and understanding.

Even if you are not a believer it will not hurt to humbly ask for help from anyone who may be out there in space just open your heart, and answers will come.

Try to begin to change your attitude with positive affirmations:

> I can do this. I am wise enough and have enough energy.
>
> I can do anything I put my mind to do.
>
> I am capable.
>
> I will enlist the help of my own family to assist me.
>
> I will research to find added help that is available.

This will add to my life and not deplete me.

Repetition is the mother of all learning, so practice, practice, and practice.

Whatever you affirm in your mind will culminate in your actions. You become an expression of those affirmations.

Dump the words I can't, I won't, I don't want to, I don't know how, etc. Those are self-defeating terms so if you find yourself beginning to say one of them, practice switching over to a positive term.

It is easier than you think once you get in the habit of doing it.

The truth is we all have to share in the same process and progressions of life. Aging and dying are a common denominator for all mankind.

Do not allow the knowledge you gain to slip away. Use your knowledge to make someone else's life a bit easier, and you will ultimately improve your own life. You will find maturity and wisdom blossoming from within, and it will make your tomorrows easier. This is another promise

I make! I am grateful for what I learned while care giving my little Mama.

This last year has been the most demanding physically and mentally for me, and I believe if I had not learned so much while helping Mama, I might have ended up in an asylum. Seriously.

With insights learned and wisdom applied, and giving thanks and credit to God, I have been carried through on the wings of an angel, and am endeavoring to find peace in the new me.

Be honest with the person you are caring for if you wear down. Gently remind them it has added to your workload but you are willing because you love them.

When I told Mama that I think she was inspired to keep a sweeter attitude even in rough times, which in turn really helped me pull through. I think her strength grew to help me along the way.

See if you can develop and keep that zest for living by seeing from your heart and appreciating even the smallest blessings.

With each heartbeat no matter how exhausted I was, I knew this was my position, and I chose to be good at what I was doing.

Think of such things as how miraculous it is that we can breathe and move, and how we are able to perceive, conceive, compute, heal, and achieve.

Be aware of the wonderful things we often take for granted. Listen to the sound of the leaves blowing in the wind, the song of the birds in springtime, and the sound of rain pelting the roof in a storm.

Divert your Mama's attention from her aches and pains, grab her hand and make her listen and watch too.

Sometimes pain can distract you from these wonderful gifts that anyone can enjoy. These small things may be the most wonderful moments your mama can enjoy.

Take time to thank God for everything that is good. No matter what our disadvantage or problem, our biggest handicap is our own response!

If you do not believe in God, keep an open mind. There is not a human on the planet that has not called upon God for help at some point.

When the crisis comes these words, "Oh God", are voiced across the planet. See if you can practice calling on God moment to moment. You may find the empty place in your heart that you seek to be filled, belonged to God all along.

Remember love quiets anxiety. A soft voice draws peace near it. Love will lift you above any challenge you may meet along the way. Love never fails. You as a caregiver have the opportunity to change the life of a person who has no dreams and is facing what may be terrifying to them – death.

Though the term caregiver has carried a negative connotation you will find that ultimately, in giving you will receive so much more than you gave.

I once read young children are pressed freshly from the mind of heaven and are still sensitized with the imprint of thedivine seal of joy and enthusiasm, for them to circulate, share and reveal from within. I was taken by the author's words though I do not know who penned them. What a statement of love, and how true it is.

As adults we become desensitized and forget that spontaneous joy and love we once felt. Life caves in on us and often we become dependent on our outer circumstances to dictate whether we feel joy or happiness.

Do not let this happen to you. It is a choice. Insist on a joyous attitude. Be a cheerful giver.

Fake it if you have to at first. Getting into the habit of joy takes practice if it is new to you. Practice. Spontaneous joy and happiness will become habit, it will come to fruition.

We create our lives even though time and circumstances that happen to us all. We are still responsible for our thoughts and our words, hence our actions. CREATE a masterpiece of your life for yourself by forging though one of the most difficult, and one of the most rewarding jobs, as that of a caregiver.

Do it with fervor and draped in love.

Brighten the way for your Mama and lighten her load. We are always FREE to make right and loving choices.

Be forgiving of yourself, and the person you are caring for, all the days it is your position.

Being a caregiver can be a position of honor and will help shape and define what you do today and tomorrow. Take a breath, say a prayer, smile and get on with the tasks at hand.

Mama often said to me:

"Be a light in the darkness honey. You know even the smallest light in the darkness changes everything."

Addendum

I have been told this book is s a love story between a mother and a daughter. I know that is true in part. I did love my mother and felt totally blessed she was a little spitfire who loved her children more than anything else in the world.

I also learned so much from caring for her during her last years I felt it urgent to share some of the knowledge we attained together.

Your job as a caregiver will be to make her life a joy and not go insane at the same time.

No one ever said this job would be an easy one. I was fortunate as Mama was a very unusual person and interesting as well.

She made her share of mistakes in life, so do not misunderstand my accolades. I had made more than my share of mistakes myself!

We are all human. But where Mama excelled was in _**her unconditional love and loyalty**_. I think she would have traded her sharp intellect for a healthier body those last years, but I feel very fortunate she remained sharp. I think it made the whole position much easier.

She had multiple injuries, was born with her hip out of the socket, and also had osteoporosis, a terrible disease. She understood. She fully comprehended and accepted what life had become the last years of her life. How fortunate was that for me!

I also want to mention, if you were not so lucky, and really don't like your Mama – at least help find her someone else who can care for her. If you cannot forgive and forget what cause the breech between you, do not torture her with your own anger and unforgiving emotions. She has enough hardships to handle.

By holding on to grudges and not forgiving, in actuality you do more damage to yourself than to anyone else! Believe it, as it is true.

Be realistic and follow be your best self. We can only do in this life, what we are capable of doing, or learning.

Keep in mind though; usually we are capable of so much more than we give ourselves credit for and in vast areas of human growth.

If you find yourself willing to care for her because of your own life responsibilities, enlist a family member, other close relatives, or even children who are willing to pitch and help. Admit you need help.

There are also many more services to help your mama now that the information highway is in full bloom. Knowledge is power, and help is available.

God bless you in this diverse and difficult task. Remember, please:

IT COULD BE YOU IN THE FUTURE THAT NEEDS HELP!

Be credible and loving. As you give, so shall you receive.

Mama had a favorite poem. I would like to share it with you. It is as true today as when she first read it to me:

INVICTUS

"Out of the night that covers me,

Black as the Pit from pole to pole,

I thank whatever gods may be

For my unconquerable soul."

"In the fell clutch of circumstance

I have not winced nor cried aloud.

Under the bludgeoning of chance"

My head is bloody, but unbowed."

"Beyond this place of wrath and tears

Looms but the Horror of the shade.

And yet the menace of the years

Finds, and shall find, me unafraid."

"It matters not how strait the gate,

How charged with punishments the scroll.

I am the master of my fate:

I am the captain of my soul."

William Ernest Henley

Her heart touched my heart. Mama's wisdom and words still ring true. Now it has been over twenty-five years since she left us all.

Every moment with her is now a memory of gold. Though I felt overwhelmed at times, I am so glad I gave her joy in her last years on this planet. She gave me much more.

She has not left me. The Spirit of her love dwells within me, and I am certain we shall meet again.

Lovingly written,

Marsha J. O'Brien

The Holy Bible, containing The Old

and

New Testaments,

in the King James Version.

The New Open Bible Study Edition

Copyright 1990 by Thomas Nelson,

Inc.

-----

of seeing Mama that way. I also let go of the guilt. Michael simply said I was not supposed to be there. I finally agreed.
